The Place Where Wildness Dreams

Essays from the Field

Alexis Rykken

The Place Where Wildness Dreams:
Essays from the Field

Printed in the United States of America

For information, contact Nighthawk Press:
www.nighthawkpress.com

ISBN: 978-0692323403
Library of Congress Control Number: 2014955561

Cover photograph © René Janiece
Design: Barbara Scott, Final Eyes, Barb@FinalEyes.net
Author photograph by René Janiece

The back-cover photo was taken at Stateline Road, between Colorado and New Mexico, outside Jaroso, Colorado. If you trace the road west to where it ends, you overlook the place where the magnificent Río Grande Gorge begins, at the northernmost border of our newly designated Río Grande del Norte National Monument in New Mexico. This primitive site – untamed, unpeopled – graces our front cover.

www.nighthawkpress.com

"We are honored to include Alexis as a featured thinker in residence in the Thinking Wilderness Project, and invite you to travel, through her words, into the wilds of your imagination and then perhaps into wilderness itself."

— ANITA MCKEOWN & CLAIRE COTÉ
Creative Directors, Thinking Wilderness Project
LEAP (Land, Experience and Art of Place)
www.leapsite.org

"In *The Place Where Wildness Dreams,* Alex Rykken explores the heart-call of the land, giving voice to her love affair with the natural world. In prose as vibrant and authentic as the wild itself, she examines integrity as the heart and soul of wilderness. Alex encourages the reader not only to walk with her on her pilgrimage but to heed the call of their own."

— RENÉ JANIECE, singer/songwriter, *Bittersweet Highway*

"This is straight from the body writing — instinctual, sensuous. Alex's stories sing with the call of coyote, the holy tenacity of wolf and sandhill crane, the dreams of untamed hearts. Her powerful observations in the field are interwoven with her love and deep respect for the land."

— JILL BACHMAN, graphic design/editor
A Field Guide — Through the Eyes of Children,
Bosque del Apache National Wildlife Refuge

"…a lyrical read that captures the beauty and essence of wildness in the forest, the desert, the rivers, and ourselves."

— REBECCA WILLIAMS, naturalist/educator

Dedicated to my Gypsy Soul,
the bone and soul spirit of wilderness,
and to
Thomas Berry for
The DREAM of the EARTH

Acknowledgments

This year, we celebrate the 50-year anniversary of the signing of the Wilderness Act by President Johnson. This book is a thank-you to all who work for wilderness, and to all wild ones on the edge of civilization dreaming Earth wild.

This collection of essays is a tribute to the Red River Valley in North Dakota, and the small river town where I grew up.

The Place Where Wildness Dreams is a paean to my gypsy soul. She is the author of my pilgrimage. This book, this walk, is her ground. She drops me off where the path leads, leaving me vulnerable, raw, open. I venture out to find the stories, the power of the holy fire beneath the surface, the dream.

Each new place becomes a study. The place where I walk…and listen…and write.

The stories, the places, form a territory, a mandala: Drayton, North Dakota. Lankin, North Dakota. Evergreen, Colorado. Ely, Minnesota. Bluff, Utah. Magdalena, New Mexico. Kanab, Utah. San Antonio, New Mexico. Flagstaff, Arizona. Woody Creek, Colorado. Taos, New Mexico. Mancos, Colorado. Farmington, New Mexico. Ojo Caliente, New Mexico. Saguache, Colorado. Jaroso, Colorado.

I offer my heartfelt thanks to my editor, Barbara Scott, who, steady as a rock, collaborated with me, as one would with a feral kitten. Her attention to the "little picture" is an act of love — for the language and the writer.

To my good friend Susan Wilcox, who rescued this manuscript from the dark abyss of computer hell — thank you for saving my story.

And to all who follow their soul's call, the hidden strange uncertainty at bedrock, walk on.

Contents

Water Catches Light

Foreword

Brilliant. Sustained. Here — as very few books can deliver — is an authenticity you will quickly recognize. *The Place Where Wildness Dreams* is powerful in moments, prayerful throughout. Important to the point of being vital. I found myself walking with the author, riveted by Elk, Bear and Spider, traveling at a pace I had not anticipated. I found myself on a pilgrimage I'll not forget. For this is a work of intimacy; a generous feast of passion, adventure and participation greet me in ways I've not found before, perhaps in ways I thought impossible, in ways I've always wanted.

"Come, walk with me," the author invites.

All the world is here — from Bear to Rabbit, from Jaguar to Pica, from Mountain to Valley. The beings of the desert, the prairie, the forests and skies all reside with us, in a place that is both "out there" and within. The distant is brought near. And that which is too close to see is made visible. *The Place Where Wildness Dreams* enters Earth's dream, offers a new sensibility of who we are as part of an integral community, opens our minds to the consciousness of the natural world. As a reader, you join the author's innate sense of journey…and you find in your own gypsy soul that this journey is not one you are just starting, nor will it end with the final page.

William Howell

Introduction

*The gift of pilgrimage is a love affair carefully tended,
a walk into the Holy Labyrinth of wild country, each step a
pause, a story along the way, circling, circling toward the
core. Listening for the old wisdom.*

I grew up on an inland sea, rocked to sleep by prairie songs. The music of a vast living land sounds in the deepest territory of my heart. Rivers flowing wild. A blast of wind roaring through the night, sheets of rain beating a rhythm on wooden shingles, the crash of thunder, lightning splitting dark skies sizzling over ground. Whiteout blizzards sweeping in from the north, burying the land in silence.

I grew up in the Red River Valley in North Dakota, where the far view extends to forever. When I was a child, I lived my days outdoors. I roamed the shores of the Red River, open to the changing mysteries waiting around each curve. I rode my bike far into the countryside seeking an energy I could not name. I did not know then the words ecology or integrity. I followed the language of my deepest heart.

I have lost my way many times in this world of grown-up distractions and desires, yet that young child's endurance calls me back: approaches, opens doorways, challenges me.

* * *

Backpacking into the Río Grande National Forest, I follow a rutted path meandering along the río, climbing toward Stony Pass in the Rocky Mountains of Colorado, headwaters of the great river.

A young bobcat races toward me, running flat out, low to the ground. I stumble off trail. My hand grips the dog's collar, pulling him along beside me. A huge black bear streaks around the bend through heat waves where the energy of the cat still flickers. I feel a rush of air as the bear passes by. His scent lingers.

All is quiet.

The uncanny thing is how silently the two creatures vanish into the canyon, yet their presence commands the space where I stand. Silver shards of light, a full-out shimmer of atoms and molecules, hang in the air, rustled up by the two animals moving through. Each golden leaf, the sound of water tumbling over stone, the curved angle of the trail, minute crevices in canyon walls: all fall into sharp detail, charged with energy.

It is here, in this unexpected moment, that my story takes a turn. This brush with integrity ignites a hunger. I am hungry for expression, hungry for the long meander.

And so I go. I head out first to the vast desert and canyon lands of the Southwest at a time when all is open.

My various packs of dogs are my most frequent and exuberant companions — just us and all the faraway before us. I place my boots on ground, where earth articulates a hauntingly beautiful language, subtle and strong and life giving as breath. A pulse sultry as a cat's purr echoes from the canyon floor. Intricate rhythms sweep out of shadowy crags and ridges. A primeval chaos of folded and faulted and uplifted rock formations generate a complex beat all their own, shimmering, radiating molten fire. Red-gold cliffs, plants, animals, the furred, winged and scaled gather here to dream. Hidden in caves, ancient bear and cougar shift their bones in sleep. Dreams rumble over dusty stone. Each dream originates from deep in the center of the earth. Not a single dream is lost.

Anything I want to know is rooted in the land. If I allow my thoughts and expectations to be still long enough, I may understand something of the way the land speaks. I may remember how to be a part of earth's dream.

I have become a wanderer with a penchant for the lands where desert rattlesnakes perform their ritual dance, where light holds a presence. I am witness to my own story, a blood memory called down from my Scandinavian ancestors who knew the natural world as the extraordinary world, as the place of spirit. Packing my gear — walking the trail — is my work, the necessity of my life. It is what allows me to live.

I am indebted to natural-history scribes, poets, cultural historians, Native American authors, scientists, my ancestors, and others, who recognize earth as a conversationalist, a living, breathing system, interconnected and fluid. Their passion sets me firmly back on track when I doubt my own path, when I feel as if my soul will break.

I am particularly indebted to Thomas Berry for his clarity in recognizing the human community's need to participate in Earth's dream. In *The Dream of the Earth,* Berry asks the fundamental question of how life can continue to evolve on this planet. He suggests that we listen to what the earth has to tell us about itself as a self-organizing process governed by what he terms the primordial dream whence all things come into being.

* * *

I write to know the places I walk, tattered pages carried in my backpack, aligning myself to what I deeply love. The genesis for this book was a simple desire to consolidate my stack of journals into one. In calling up images of my meandering I have settled into a contemplative writing pace. I want the integrity of wilderness — the dreams of fellow creatures, moments of personal experience — to speak of vulnerability, beauty, territory, and the primal spirit of the land.

I have moved slowly with this writing, listening carefully, pressing past my own walls to the place where Earth's dreams take hold. As a rock cairn marks a pathway, each story marks a resting place along the way, a touchstone, and a journey's range. The enigma of my journey, the gift, emerges as the language of the sensuous world — lush or spare; quiet or raucous; liquid, vegetable, or mineral; feathered or furred or scaled; raging or demure — reveals integrity in each wild body, intelligence attuned to the complex design of life on this planet.

Benedicto:

May your trails be crooked,
winding, lonesome,
dangerous, leading to the most amazing view.
May your mountains rise into and above the clouds.
May your rivers flow without end,
meandering through pastoral valleys
tinkling with bells,
past temples and castles and poets' towers
into a dark primeval forest where
tigers belch and monkeys howl,
through miasmal and mysterious swamps
and down into a desert of red rock,
blue mesas, domes and pinnacles and
grottos of endless stone,
and down again into a deep vast
ancient unknown chasm
where bars of sunlight blaze on profiled cliffs,
where deer walk across the white sand beaches,
where storms come and go
as lightning clangs upon the high crags,
where something strange and more beautiful
and more full of wonder than your
deepest dreams waits for you — beyond
that next turning of the canyon walls."

EDWARD ABBEY

Walking the Far Boundaries of Home

There is a story, always ahead of you.
Barely existing. Only gradually do you attach
yourself to it and feed it.

Michael Ondaatje
The Cat's Table

No one suspects the days to be gods.

RALPH WALDO EMERSON

Of Wind, Water, and Song

Annie Dillard writes in *The Writing Life*, "We still and always want waking. We should amass half dressed in long lines like tribesmen and shake gourds at each other, to wake up; instead we watch television and miss the show."

We live in a spirited world. All around us the gods are awake. Wolf, Grizzly, Prairie Dog, Lynx, Frog. The trees. The rivers. Just one sweet dog or cat. The light in their eyes carries an unfathomable depth of knowing. The light in their eyes will take you down to your knees to see, waking up that bitter, sharp, hard kernel at the core. You can no longer abide compression. Cannot abide holding the frantic "I'm sooo busy," the superior affectations we cling to.

Cell by cell, molecule by molecule, we change; the old kernel cracks, opens. Our bodies remember simply being present to the song, moving with the grace of flowing water.

West of town, a prairie-dog village holds my attention. I know that beneath the ground, their tunnels flow outward in all directions for perhaps a quarter mile or more. Petals of flowers, pine boughs and down line their burrows. A tenderness in the earthy darkness. There is a vitality in these colonies, uncontrived, refreshing, peaceful — elegant in a way. Babies are out of their burrows today; adults mingle with them, playing, teaching, and grooming in a calm manner. Fully attentive. Their voices carry across the meadow as music. Sentinels stand in place, watchful, alert. Two red-tailed hawks circle the village, shrieking a blood-chilling call. Alarm rings out. The colony scurries underground.

Nearby, a female coyote naps in her quiet cliffside den. Songbirds, a symphony of motion, sweep into the brush. Bullfrogs mumble in the depths of a faraway marsh. Canada geese nest in the rough grasses cradling the marsh. Blue jays, ravens, eagles soar in skies of deepest blue. All hold their place in nurturing creation, their work a lovely mosaic of balance. The intelligence in each small body, their complex lives, their value to the planet, astonish my mind.

Facing the sun, I stand as the little dogs do, hands raised in prayer, as our communities disappear.

Our footprint on this planet is heavy and relentless. Most of us exist in a world we do not comprehend. We are bewildered by the intricate relationships, the mystery, the overwhelming complexity of the natural world, the territorial boundaries. Most of us are asleep to the utter beauty we live within. We hide our sorrow, our ignorance, our bewilderment, in intellectual or spiritual pursuits — or we go insane with grief.

Some years ago, I worked with a group of fellows who had initiated a study of the Río Grande. We did not realize at the time how the wild inhabitants of the earth would lead us to a world of complex relationships whose lives insure the survival of our planet. The force of their presence, the substance of their environment, became our world, too. We pushed ourselves to follow the faint or bright tracks of life on the río. An energy consumed us, tender in its care. Discussions emerged spontaneously. Our study came alive through art. Mandalas, mosaics, murals emerged as the visionary work of shamans, primal in their shape and form. A world of mystery came through.

Osprey's brushy nest cradles two chicks, just visible. Red-tailed Hawk's predatory dive holds us in her spell. Ghosts of Grizzly Bear fish for trout high up on the mountain. Coyote's extraordinary eyes reveal dreams for Earth. Trout, her sleek shape, her rainbow-colored scales, carry memories of mountains turned to grains of sand...of water catching light. Prairie Dog, buff-colored monks of the field, send out their share of hope. Frog, Turtle, Snake recall río's graceful meander, her cool muddy shores. Beetle creates pyramids of soil, allowing moisture to escape. Owl calls down blankets of starlight. Sandhill Crane, timeless in grace, flies full circle back to the beginning and beyond.

"The world is filled, and filled with the Absolute," Teilhard de Chardin wrote. "To see this is to be made free."

Walking the Far Boundaries of Home

All stories begin with the breath.

My first breath, my first story: the cool, sweet air of the Northern Plains. Farm country: golden fields, wetlands, skies dipping over the horizon to places unknown. I grew up in a small town set on the banks of the Red River of the North. When I was young, the Red River was an untamed power. Foreboding. In winter, huge jagged ice floes, heaped in mounds of snow, sprang out of the frozen river as monsters of the deep. In spring, muddy waters rampaged over the prairie, turning streets into canals, flooding our basements, our houses.

When the river receded, the ground was waterlogged and altered, the landscape roughed up and cold. Trees were down, gigantic roots exposed to the air clotted with dirt and debris, a sight both monstrous and vulnerable. The heavy scent of soggy hay and soaked earth drifted over the prairie. The river pulled long, dark gray clouds out of the sky. Mist hovered over the tips of field grasses. On these misty cool days I rode my bike away from town, following dirt roads curving into the distance, my mind alert to the voices of the land. Out there in that great wide distance, I became something wild, a secret wildness called forth from somewhere deep inside. I knew the running deer, the soaring hawk, and the fox safely hidden in his cozy den. I felt their presence, their invisibility.

The blood of the Northern Plains runs through my veins, steadies me, holds me to the ground. I carry in my heart the secret I knew as a child — a feral instinct essential to my soul.

* * *

This morning, my dogs and I explore the far boundaries of our home in southwestern Colorado, where the Rocky Mountains show off their tallest peaks. The Sangre de Cristo Range to the east and the San Juan Mountains to the west have long been wise old traveling companions, etching stories in the deepest shadows of my heart. In my case, it was love at first sight; a heart-pounding rambunctious passion for this landscape took hold and never let go.

Walking the quiet of this early-September morning, I trudge along a deer trail through a patchy aspen grove as one who belongs, silent and wary, to experience again the energy I find only in wilderness.

All of wild nature sends a gift, a resounding pulse streaming through the universe, a power song straight to the womb, an intimacy I crave. Layers of geology's rocks and crystals reveal stories of timelessness. Ice and swirling snow, harsh rainstorms, underground springs, fast-moving creeks, animals and plants expose a core integrity, reminding me that I am in the presence of a fierce beauty not to be taken for granted. Circulating mists shadow the face of the mountain. Ghost roads flow in all directions. A double-track trail leads into the valley.

The valley floor extends for thousands of square miles, an intricate mandala of cottonwood and willow, rolling hills, windblown dunes, streams, small homes and ranch land. The valley's voice is lush, carrying stories of the truly sensuous: wind, water and sand.

I walk toward a still-sleeping hillside where Coyote holds council. We, my dogs and I, understand our relationship here. We each have territories to patrol, and conversations must be had. We understand that we are the visitors and Coyote the grand master, the forever Hunter Shaman.

Behind our house, Cottonwood Creek flows clear and cold, moving down the mountain from her birthplace in the icy tundra, a timeless rhythm of active, whirling, spiraling forms — Earth's blood. Emerald-green moss grows thick along the banks of Cottonwood Creek. Waves and ripples mark the sandy shore. Tracks of furred and feathered and scaled tell stories of the night before. Riffles and swirls race down the mountain, polishing stones nestled in the sandy creek bed.

My three cats join us for this short walk. Exuberant, dazzled by the ethereal element of water, they leap to climb the highest tree. Padding across branches arching over the creek, their graceful bodies are as supple and fluid as the dancing water deities calling to them.

We are water — 78 percent of our bodies, 90 percent of our brains. If it's true that the landscape forms the mind, I choose the mind of water, the fluid element, the element that keeps us from becoming too rigid. We, each one of us, nurtured by our mother's body, are cradled in a sphere of water.

The imprint of water's spiraling forms can be found in the structure of our bones and muscles and organs. The energy of water carries the truth of who we are. Enter the mind of water and you, too, become infinite, powerful, ever changing, moving through or around or over every obstacle.

Last week, my dogs and I walked a jeep road angling high into the mountains. We had just rounded a curve, the place of the drop-off on one side and the steep cliff on the other, when we met a cinnamon-colored black bear heading our way. We all stopped. My dogs sat down and turned to stone. The bear sat down. We were at an impasse. Where to go? My big dog, Charley, huffed several times, indicating he was scared. The bear returned the huffing sound. We were all scared! And yet my mind stayed alert, cognizant of the bear's energy, the grace-ful power held in his body. His coat was fluffed, bristling in the light. He looked huge. His total concentration was on us. I looked into his eyes. Curious possibly? Surprised? Yes. Perhaps he had, just moments ago, walked out of the dense camouflage of the forest to find himself exposed here on this old road. And who should he meet? Us! I cast my eyes downward. I took a deep breath. I shifted my head to the side, exposing my neck (a non-aggressive stance understood by bears) communicating that we did not wish to fight. The bear lowered his head in the same manner. We were all holding our own. Then, with great dignity, he stretched, turned toward the cliff and was out of sight in an instant.

Most wild creatures are private, shy, and partial to remaining unseen. All manner of the wild call this place home offering the presence of unfathomable majesty. In rare moments, we are fortunate to experience untainted wilderness, a full heart teaching, an open door to a more-than-human world. This larger world, the beyond-human world, reveals the complex ecology of integrity. True community. If we choose to cross this threshold, we enter the dream of the earth. The natural world lives from this place, immersed in a delicate, intricate, territorial balance. More and more wildlife habitat now includes the human element. Life is dependent on our understanding the intelligence, the language, the contribution of our fellow inhabitants.

It is fall in the Sangre de Cristos. Today my dogs and I follow a trail leading into the high country. Lacy crystals of ice layer the creek. Aspens shimmer gold in the basins. Out of the sunlit distance of memory, caught in the shining light, a young girl appears as a mirage. She walks toward us, her hair golden as the turning leaves. We meet as old friends. We walk together through the dreaming place of bears. We reach the heart of the mountain, where rumpled brown earth has taken on the shape of sleeping bears. We listen to their song on the breath of the wind.

This turning toward what you deeply love saves you.

RUMI

At Bedrock...Integrity

I was a young mother when my grandmother died. She was ninety-two years old. Two days before her death I dreamed of her. In the dream I was a child, perhaps eight years old, sitting up in bed pillows piled around me. I wore red flannel pajamas. My grandmother's chair was pulled up beside my bed. The chair looked like a golden throne. Grandmother was wearing a plain white cotton nightgown. Her face was the face of a wild animal. She was telling me a story, so I knew this was my grandmother, although she wore an animal face. Perhaps it is a mask, I thought. In her arms, she cradled a tiny bear cub. I could see she loved this baby very much. She looked straight into my eyes. "When I die you must care for the cub."

My grandmother, my wild-spirited ancestor. I have not always remembered to care for the precious gift she entrusted me—an ages old intelligence offered as a responsibility. I have not always remembered to guard with tenderness Earth's wild spirit or my own. I have found distractions aplenty. Developing a partnership with the natural world, staying true to my own wild spirit, is a gut-level commitment, a lonely, conflicted commitment in a world where "dominance over" is the worldview.

My grandmother carried in her soul a primal presence, a beautiful depth, compelling and mysterious. She was the storyteller at the bonfire, a seer. She instilled in me a raw unquenchable longing for wilderness.

Her legacy, rooted deep, recalls the most ancient form of prayer, the simple act of walking. I've found the deepest form of satisfaction in this prayerful practice.

During the time my family lived in northern Minnesota, she visited often. I awaited her visits eagerly. My memory of her begins when I was just three years old.

* * *

Our ritual is always the same. We greet sunrise with a walk along the shore of the Lake of the Woods. In the stillness of a misty morning, we watch moose paddle far out in the lake until just their heads and large ungainly antlers are visible above water. An eagle coasts over the deep waters, huge wingbeats pushing air, sharp eyes alert for movement. Suddenly, in a flash of light Eagle drops out of the sky, wings uplifted, talons extended to grab a large pike for breakfast. The heavy fish, clutched in Eagle's strong grip, struggles for its life as the two sail together through the air toward the cliffs.

A line of quicksilver dances over the lake, Canada geese seeking refuge on their long migration south.

Curious bright red cardinals perch on pine branches. Red birds, we call them. When I hold out my hand, offering toast crumbs, they fly so close I can almost touch their black feathered faces. Tiny nuthatches sleep in tree holes. Golden crowned kinglets gather on willow branches singing their high-pitched *kee kee.*

One morning a wolf crosses a sandbar, pauses, turns to look in our direction, amber eyes magnifying light. My heart skips a beat, and I stand transfixed by something I only know deep in my soul. Her coat ruffles in the breeze, all shades of gold and brown and black. In one leap, the wolf reaches the far shore. She lifts her voice to the sky and the world stops.

"How wonderful," I hear my grandmother whisper. On these walks she introduces me to the land spirits who live in the forest. She shows me how to see their wizened old faces in rocks and trees. *Dísir,* she calls them. A Swedish word for guardian spirits.

My paternal grandmother: there was this quality she had, a depth of knowing carried with grace and humility. "Remember, little girl," she would say, "walk softly. Watch for the old ones." During her long life, when we were together our time was spent in whatever untouched place in nature we could find. And yes, the spirits were there, all around. I find them in some places even today.

My grandmother knew and spoke of an older self, a self that will outlast the body. "This older self is the best part of you," she would say. "This older self knows the ordinary world as the extraordinary world." "Remember." "Walk softly, little girl. Listen for the song."

We are intimately connected to wilderness.
If we remembered this, our hearts
would heal. We would know magic.

Tracks in the Sand

Keeping…time…with…the rhythm of the land. Keeping…time…with…the cycling of the stars, the spell of mother moon. Keeping…time…with… the howl of a winter blizzard, night winds curling chilly fingers around the corners of my tent. Keeping…time…with… the compelling vision of wolf, the whisper of a flower, the innocence of fresh fallen snow.

Keeping…time…with…bears and blooms, canyons and water holes. Keeping…time… with…birds and mountains and old-growth forests. Keeping…time…with…fog rising over a deep blue lake.

I hike a rough jeep trail in Sugarite Canyon. A blur of motion to my right catches my eye. I turn in time to see a black bear shove two tiny cubs up into the branches of a juniper tree.

Danger! She signals to her twins as she pushes them to safety. Danger! She signals as she pushes them out of sight. She turns to run toward a series of forested hills calling attention to herself. The babies, too young to understand her warning, tumble down from the tree, two tiny balls of fur, and scramble up the hill after her. I stand still and watch. Again, as I often do, when I hike a remote trail, I see Bear.

Mythology links Bear and Woman. Mysterious. Interconnected. Invisible. Tracks in the sand reveal our presence. I am no stranger to her world. One long hike into her territory awakens my soul. I throw off my tired old mask. What is it here that tells me I belong?

Endangered. Empowered. Which will I choose? I could let go the nightmare of our cemented world. I could choose magic, of course.

That night back in camp, I dream of Bear. In the cold silence of night, she scratches on the door to my house. The dogs bark. The door opens. She stands on the threshold. Stars fall around her down to the ground. She is not small. In her arms she carries a mask. She holds the mask out toward me. The mask is a mirror image of my face. The bear turns. She drops the mask and walks away into the darkness, leaving the shattered pieces of the mask on the ground.

So there is no going back.

So there was no going back; she had to
fight for survival among the mysteries of life

CLARICE LISPECTOR
An Apprenticeship

Walking the Mystery

The word "animal" comes from the Latin root *anima,* soul. An animal in her natural surroundings reflects soul, vitality. Her body reveals interrelatedness, authenticity. She cannot live where machines rip open the ground, where development pollutes her streams, where houses claim her territory. Fragmented and wounded, soul retreats. Bear is gone. Wolf is gone. Fox. Eagle… A street or lane may be named after her. A sculpture appears on a plaza. A shop carries animal totems.

A journey beyond the personality requires courage. The intention, the illusion of control, vanishes; the linear world disappears. Your meandering spirit breathes your body whole as you dive deep into the world of your animal heart. Opening to a larger world you are at bedrock. In the core of your being, on the most fundamental level, wildness waits to be reclaimed. A territory immensely beautiful, intimidating, unsentimental, rough and fierce, fragile in its wholeness, vulnerable to exploitation. A territory of great depth, worthy of protection.

So be still. Be here, my friend. Allow the deepening. Shatter the mask. Let the pieces fall where they may, tend to each piece as a gift. Stories come alive, as a mosaic, a labyrinth, a mandala. Fluid as a free-flowing river. Strip the veneer, strip the dirt and grime layer by layer. The social mask takes so much energy. This work is not about you, or me. Each step we take into the mystery is a return to authenticity.

Where are we if we walk away from our commitment to mystery and beauty? Where are we if we walk away from the sustaining power of Earth's vision?

Today I watch a black bear play in a field of prairie grasses near a stream in the foothills of the Sangre de Cristo Mountains. She is young—charmed by the flight of a butterfly. She moves as a dancer. Her cinnamon coat ripples in waves, a melody in symphony with butterfly, meadow and the flowing stream, all shades of gold and amber and silver. Here are Bear's colors. Here is Bear's home, her shelter, her food. Newly arrived since yesterday, parked across the way, sit two bulldozers, so out of place in this fluid world. A pain like lightning shoots through my body. What now?

I am reminded that, in mythology, Bear is the caretaker who opens gateways so that we may see. Shattering the mask. Picking up the pieces. Our work starts here. We all wear the scars of experience. Some wounds are fresh still. Be there. Let your journey grow, opening to your own unplanned odyssey.

Mary Oliver writes in Wild Geese. "You do not have to be good. You do not have to crawl on your knees for a hundred miles through the desert repenting. You only have to let the soft animal of your body love what it loves."

I walk to know this place in my body…this place where wildness dreams.

So walk on my friend. Walk deep into the territory of your soul. Walk on into the mystery. Walk on, each step a prayer.

*Go into yourself and see how deep
the place is from which your life flows.*

RAINER MARIA RILKE

Gypsy Soul

Wherever I travel the backcountry of the South-western deserts I come across images on walls of sandstone...on granite faces of gigantic boulders standing as sentinels...in river canyons near the old cliff villages of the Anasazi. Sometimes when I climb to the top of a mellow hillside, I am surprised by a pyramid of rocks alive with figures: energy so present the artists could be taking a break in the shade under the trees just around the bend.

Multitudes of images — sun and serpents, spirals, warriors and gods, semi-human figures, animals — carved, pecked, others painted. Each one is a reminder of continuity. Continuity: We Are Here.

Can you reach back in your blood and hear the voices of your ancestors? Listen. At bedrock, at your core, you will find energy connected to the dreaming of the earth. At the deepest level of your being, you will find an energy nourished by Earth's dreams. At the deepest level, you will find your instinctive, intuitive essence, a point of intricacy as subtle as a baby's breath. At the deepest level, you will find your wild voice, your passion.

In a world of too much hurry it is Gypsy's call I hear, a presence within I do not fully understand yet am compelled to follow. However ancestral codes join and comingle, it is Gypsy who sprang forth this round. With her there is no question of journey. Her nomadic soul draws me inward to layers of instinct, to the place where I crave hot desert sun, meandering rivers, crimson canyon land, sage-covered hills, tall grass prairies. Gypsy brings me home to the dark rich ground from which life flows. Following Gypsy, my body remembers movement grounded in earth and wild grace.

Gypsy challenges me to walk distant edges. She challenges me to walk the holy labyrinth toward its fiery center.

How do I describe this primal place? This place of integrity where, illusive as desert light, Jaguar births her cubs in a cave above a slip of stream. Rivers run cold and deep. Wolf marks her territory, calls her pack to the hunt. Eagle gently lifts off to fly toward a golden-hued mountain. Snake curves over ground like a shadow, disappearing into his den, and Coyote hoots the full moon silver. In this place of integrity, a female grizzly slumbers in her sturdy lair.

Gypsy shows up in my dreams. She calls up blood memories; she is a reminder of my birthright. She is the quiet place within, connected to the breath. How do I find this place? I ask. "Slow down," she laughs, "walk with me."

Gypsy walks on ground where great gray wolves nurse their young, where baby otter swim and play in cold clear rivers, where beaver build their homes. She walks where rainbow bridges lead to glittering star worlds.

Gypsy walks the razor-sharp edge of the abyss, willing me to spiral deep into the wild center of Earth's great heart, into the shadow, to the unknown layers of my own body. She carries a difficult message: Be patient. Wait here. This is who you are.

For a time I struggle to belong, to live my soul's life within the narrow boundaries of society. I ache with the congestion of it all.

Eventually, I remove the mask of the good girl. Arrrrgh! With great care, I shake out my crumpled animal heart.

Gypsy unveils the soul of the medial woman and her connection to Earth's visionary spirit. She asks for a change of consciousness. Another way of being on earth. She asks for a return to intimacy with the natural world. She asks for integrity.

You may wonder how it is with Gypsy and me. Well, this is how it is. I am so conflicted. When I throw all my projections, conflicts, fears and lifestyle in a pile, it forms a mountain as tall as Mount Olympus. Often I am caught here, staring at all my stuff.

Fortunately, Gypsy stays present. She understands that it is in pushing back against boundaries that a soul is defined. As a strong wind scours the land, we become as bone — strong, enduring and luminous. Gypsy is the one who races outdoors at midnight in moonlight while fresh snow falls, to lift her hands in prayer. She is the one who hikes every hoodoo valley in Utah. She is the one who walks alone, vanishing into the mountain where Bear and Bobcat roam. She is the one who dreams tall-grass prairies where buffalo graze and prairie chickens dance. She is the one who flies in V-formation with majestic cranes on a holy migration through time. She is the one who befriends solitude as the only way to go deep. She is the one who soars alongside Golden Eagle, who knows this bright wild creature as God. She is the one who knows that the only moment is the present moment.

If I could, I would turn away and walk on, stepping forward with all my heart toward that far-flung valley at the edge of my perception, where Gypsy lives. I, however—caught in the web of important thoughts, wishes and plans—lose sight of truth.

Gypsy dreams for me. She dreams the far blue valley of my wildness, where my fears and hopes disappear into the rich dark colors of my heart; where I know the great wise Earth as my body, the clear-flowing river as my blood, the air as breath, and fire the burning passion of my visionary spirit.

The world Gypsy knows is a world where I dream Earth's dreams. Dreaming Earth wild, linear time dissolves and I am immersed in the fluid rhythms of the land.

The wild within, in the deepest sense, calls me home.

A life should have a sense of wonder, she whispers. Walk with me. Lest you forget…

There were certain powers, customs,
and ways that humans were meant to live
by. There was an order to things, a mystery
of how every single thing worked together
with the rest, merged and fitted like
it was one great body.

LINDA HOGAN
Power

Moretti's Cave

I walk out one night. I toss my dearest possessions — cell phone, laptop, iPod — into a closet. I turn away from all things distancing. I want the magic of solitude. I turn my back and shut the door. I throw my pack and sleeping gear in the back of my truck, tuck a black canvas bag under the front seat. My dogs nestle down beside me. In town, I fill the truck with gas, check the oil, the tires, and finally I stop at the ATM.

My old truck speeds through the night, windows open. My arm rests on the window sill. Cruising the high road, driving through tiny dark communities, I feel my body lighten. I hoot and howl a bit, breathe a sigh of relief. The empty road, the expansive horizon, draws me toward a place inside where I am invisible, free of personality.

I watch a new moon drift out of a cloud bank. Fresh air fills the cab. Obligations crawl under the driver's-side door and slink off to be eaten by the night. Sluggish remnants of guilt sail out the window. I hold no council with my fears. I do not look back.

Near Flagstaff, I pull into a well-lighted truck stop. I study my face in the restroom mirror. My eyes have deepened. My face seems older, more defined.

I pay for gas and coffee. Another woman, a different woman — a lean, soft-eyed woman — slides behind the wheel of the truck and drives off. Bright moonlight reflects the landscape. I enter places of great beauty. I drive on.

Just as dawn casts a sweep of crimson light over canyon walls, I stop at a café in a small town. Breakfast will be leisurely and quiet. I have no need to chat or ask questions. After all, I am invisible. From the window of the café, I watch the town awaken. Trucks and cars fill the main street. Some pull in and park in the gravel lot. Town folks enter the café. Businesspeople, ranchers, bank presidents, school teachers exchange greetings, order coffee, eat their breakfasts. I listen to soft laughter, the easygoing banter among old friends.

This is a hometown, a working town. The walls of the café hold stories of generations. I pull a pen and a small notepad out of my pocket. I list supplies and gear I will need to purchase for my stay, supplies I will need to pack into a place I remember. I will be there awhile.

* * *

Like a cat, I wake luxuriously. The fine white sand shifts under my sleeping bag, changing shape with my movement. My cave is warm, comfortable; one of many caves cut into the red rock walls rising from the floor of the canyon where the muddy river flows. I have my choice of dwellings, a kitchen here, a bedroom, a studio. Each cave has been carved and smoothed by time, wind and water. Arched doorways; soft, sandy floors; clean white adobe interiors invite the wayfarer to stay awhile. Niches in the curved walls provide natural ledges, where I place candles.

My day begins gently. Morning lights my cave. I wake to a violet-blue world. A little canyon wren's clear flutelike song pours into my chambers. Luminescent green and purple dragonflies sip from flowering plants along the river. Violet-green swallows swoop, hunting insects for youngsters snugged together in efficient mud baskets glued to sandstone walls.

Golden eagles, hawks, falcons nest in twisted juniper snags on jagged red cliffs high above the river, raptor eyes watchful. Each wild one acknowledges that I live here as a neighbor, as a sister canyon creature, unencumbered, spare.

This morning, my cave is still and dark. A rainstorm brews. Dogs nap. Dark clouds rumble low across the sky. Lightning touches ground, highlighting dark etchings on canyon walls. Desert varnish, dark lustrous stains streak red rock. The luscious smell of river mud and the happy bellow of bullfrogs sweet talk me right out of my cozy little nest.

The land carries stories.

I follow a secret path where stone cities tucked back in the labyrinth of canyons hold the presence of ancient people, strongly felt, as though they might return at any moment. Each morning, a kit fox and her young leave tiny round tracks marking the damp white sand outside my dwelling. I walk in the tracks of a graceful mountain lion, tracks larger than my footprint. I find signs of a curious bobcat who prowls the high ridges above the river. And from deep in the canyon I hear Coyote's triumphant call.

Reptiles of all sorts, fat old rattlers, the beautiful collared lizard, the rarely seen wizened old Gila monster share the land. We live together, my dogs and I, in community with our fellow canyon inhabitants.

We hike the high mesas and great canyons wearing the rich, sultry scent of sage, river and sun. A sassy coyote pup plays far out on the red dirt mesa, showing off his pouncing skills. He is coy, a grand flirt, pretending to ignore us.

Each day, I splash in the muddy Paria River. We run free of constraint, my dogs and me. I love the hard sand beneath my feet, the hot sun on my body. My feet grow large. My body carries the energy of the land, strong and open. When I choose, I sleep outside under stars, dreaming tracks across the sky. Stars and sky touch Earth in all directions. I sleep in the glow of Mother Moon. I sleep under a blanket of dark velvet encrusted with diamonds. Age-old patterns of life enliven my dreams — Callisto, lovely she-bear of the night sky; Orion; Pegasus — dreaming earth wild.

I open my canvas bag. Carefully I lay out my paints, brushes, canvas, journal.

My mind has quieted. I work from this place.

Revealing my animal heart.

Living on the edge. Digging into forgotten layers. Like me,
there are prowlers everywhere. As Abbey notes,
"…beyond the next turning of the canyon walls."

Gathering the Bones

Listening deep, I seek the luminous bone light. Raw beauty burning with grace.

Earth's stories. Stories waiting to be known.

Gathering the bones I roam, and the joy of the roaming becomes impossible to resist. There is mystery involved when giving attention to a wild place. It is here in the stillness of a place, in the soft song, the rich ground, the crackle of energy in the air. It is here rustling up images in my body — stories waiting to be known.

I carry home the bones. I listen and I wait for days or weeks. I wait to hear the story. I wait for a thought, a word, a feeling, to take wing in my heart. I wait for flesh to form, eyes to deepen, pulse to awaken. I wait for gifts of lyrical beauty, gifts of courage, gifts of love. I wait for tales of life.

Sometimes I don't catch it, and the story goes underground. Perhaps it is too painful to be told. Perhaps it will return at another time in another form. Or a story may become lost in the shadows and jostle blindly, disturbing other stories until they all clamor their way back into my heart. Sometimes I am witness to a story too hard to bear, and I am unable to face it directly. Later this story and its rippling effect will pull me toward unrealized depths, toward places I must go.

A lone jaguar crosses dangerous borders. Like a miracle, she walks out of the shadows of a cruel history to appear in the badlands of New Mexico, a vast area known as the "boot heel."

"Have you seen her?" I ask a rancher whose family has run cattle on this land for generations.

"No," he shakes his head, "but I figure if she stays around I'll catch sight of her. She could be ready to whelp. She'll settle herself a den. She'll leave signs."

"Will she be welcome?" I ask.

"You know," he says, "It all depends."

Will she be welcome? I wonder. Will she be welcome, this wild one, walking alone?

Drawn into the mystery, the harsh realities of wild country. Stripped to the bone. Bare and white and clean, I rest on sandy soil. In my bones live the ancestors. In my bones lives Earth herself. In my bones live wild creatures.

In my bones live deep rivers, stars, far reaching horizons.

In my bones lives Creation's story.

I walk one night in high-desert country. I walk through stars extending to eternity. Hidden in shadow, bones shimmer white — cradled by a sharp ridge of rose-colored limestone.

In New Mexico's high arid steppe lands, scorched by hot sun, bones shimmer white amid a sea of blue.

On a sand beach, in the belly of the gorge, camouflaged by a tangle of white driftwood, the bones rest.

One snowy day in December, I climb the Pedernal. I traverse a steep, narrow path; bones lay snugged tight against a flat flint rock, where Chipmunk chatters.

On pine shadowed ground at the foot of a lichen-covered boulder in Colorado, I find hundreds of bones. Bones of poached elk, deer, coyote.

On a rain-darkened evening in the Badlands of North Dakota, I set up camp near a muddy river. Below my camp on the shores of the river, a horned skull glistens. Buffalo. I think. I plow through foot-deep mud at midnight. The dark river roars by, threatening to overflow her banks. I lift the heavy skull in my arms, fighting for footing in sleazy mud. Returning to camp I carefully place this precious gift on a red rug in the bed of my truck.

In Arizona, outside of Kayenta, I walk across a sweep of golden prairie. Inch my way down a steep walled arroyo, tumble into a pebbled stream, and struggle through tall, dry, itchy grasses; slap mosquitoes; crawl, slip and slide up the other side of the arroyo; spit sand from my mouth only to be attacked in the foot by a cactus guarding the bones.

I scrunch through a narrow rock crevice in a hoodoo valley in southern Utah. Beyond my reach rest the bones. I twist my body like Snake. I stretch. Reaching for the stories.

On a dark paneled wall in the den of a handsome home in Texas hang the restless bones of Zebra, Hippo, Elephant, and Cougar. A coyote pelt adorns a leather ottoman. The smell of fear scents the rich furnishings in this house of betrayal.

Beneath a barbed fence in Utah, I kneel to place my hand on a small skeleton, one tiny hoof still entangled in a thorn of wire.

Exposed on a desert hillside, near a friend's home in Wyoming, once buried deep, uncovered by rain, kissed by hot sun, carried by Coyote, rocked by howling blizzards, pelted by hail. Graceful deer antlers, tipped black.

Butler Wash, Utah: I slither over waves of sun-warmed slickrock. Above me, bones rest high on a narrow ledge tucked away from prying eyes. Out of reach.

Under a brushy sage, a young diamondback curls sleepily around the bones.

*With the Desert Fathers you have the characteristic of a
clean break with a conventional, accepted social context in
order to swim for one's life into an apparently irrational void.*

THOMAS MERTON

Surrender

Yesterday I was lost most of the day. I couldn't settle in. I was hot, dusty and tired. I drove the edge of a remote desert road longing for the cool green mountains near my Colorado home. I ached to be on familiar ground. Cumulus clouds formed in the bright-blue sky.

> September, and I am falling
> falling
> like a lover
> surrendering
>
> Surrendering
> as though for the first time
> to the unknown. I play

where boundaries blend and blur
Where lavender light
becomes
violet
becomes orange liquid
on far horizons.

Thunderheads roll
storm light
heavy dark gray light
becoming rain
darts of lightning split the night.

Light turns to indigo
a brush of indigo on dark velvet
birthing a cold blue moon. Desert light
sheer light waves
piercing deep
absolute mystery.

Barry Lopez writes, "When I first came to the desert I was arrested by the space, especially what hung in a layer above the dust of the desert floor. The longer I regarded it, the clearer it became that its proportion had limits, that it had an identity, like the air around a stone. I suspected that everything I'd come here to find out was hidden inside that sheet of space."

"Will you walk with me?" Barry Lopez asks in *Desert Notes.* "Will you walk with me?" Gypsy calls from the dungeon where I have thrown her in order that I may be accommodating.

Accommodation causes me stress. I lose focus. Yet how quickly I am pulled to be accommodating. Driven by purpose and goals and a need to succeed, I shun what I know to be true for me. I harbor an urge to live the regular life I imagine others lead. When that urge leaps to the surface, I become a conflicted paunchy mess. I seek the spotlight. I hustle about wishing to be noticed. I abandon my soul, my primal ground, and ignore the outrage she feels at being betrayed.

If truth be told I am uncomfortable with my own species. My shyness is an integral part of who I am. I find serenity in the wanderer's life. I find the anonymity I seek; stripped down, bare, invisible.

"Will you walk with me?" Gypsy calls.

To walk the earth in Gypsy's shoes is both my gift and my challenge; each day she yearns to roam, to touch the primal chord existing in wild places. "Will you walk with me?" she asks. "Will you walk with me to those places where wild animals cull out their territory, piss on their boundaries, remain unseen?" A larger world. This is the reality Gypsy knows, nurtures in her body.

I struggle for words to name this territory of my soul, to give it image. Gypsy simply lives it. "Will you walk with me?" she asks. She knows I have forgotten how.

Eventually I heed her call, not realizing at first that this will cause a fall. I follow her, leaving behind the pretense of belonging. I leave to learn again from the old ones to see. I leave to hold dear my animal heart.

Today, I walk a narrow path that skirts the rim of the Río Grande Gorge. The sky is brilliant blue. I drove north through piñon country to reach this place. Violet-green swallows swoop gracefully below the canyon rim. I rest at the edge, sinking into sunbaked earth. Slowly I breathe light into my lungs, all the way to my toes. I part company with my righteous voice. My mind wanders at a leisurely pace. The path it chooses meanders a riverine course.

Song of Wild Things in Moonlight

Several years ago a health crisis, serious in its implications, appeared on my horizon. Initially, I explored the medical model; suggestions for treatment were offered. Eventually, I chose to follow a natural healing path, a revealing and difficult journey. I also chose to be quiet about this diagnosis with family or friends. I sought support from health practitioners in various fields of the healing arts. I struggled to attend to my body. I learned to listen to the wisdom of my dreams.

One restless night, I dream I am standing beside a great oak tree. In my arms I cradle a bundle of long silver spheres formed from a light, flexible metal. My dreaming self envisions placing the spheres on the ground to form a circle; but when I spontaneously let go, they fall to the ground. Each pair forms an oval. Letting go, silver spheres fall together in their own way to shape the mandorla, the mystical almond shape, a symbolic opening or gateway.

My Scandinavian ancestors understood oak groves as places of worship, of healing, where gateways open to unseen worlds. At night when I am awake and fearful, my grandmother whispers, "Listen child; listen with your heart child. A dream is calling you. Dreams old as time, they call to you."

In time I travel to a healing place with my four dogs, one cat, three down sleeping bags, a ground cloth, a tarp and one large cooler. We settle in this place of great beauty. We live with snow, sleet, rain and sunshine. We live with wild animals in this place of great beauty. I am a stranger in their home, staying here, I agree, until only the bones remain.

I gather lichen-covered stone to build a small shelter under a tall pine at the edge of the canyon. I find pleasure in creating this definition of space. My shelter opens to the elements.

I am surrounded by beauty, where deep inside my belly sorrow lives. Gradually we become feral with no effort. Our lives fall into rhythm with the place, this healing place. Black cat Persephone transforms, becomes a panther. She cuts a den into the side of a cliff. Her den has a natural rock ledge, where she stretches out to watch over her territory. She grows large. Her black fur sleek. At night she crawls into the sleeping bag with Yorkie and me.

Barney sleeps beside us, in the curve of my body, snug under a warm down blanket. Max and Hopi Girl rest on soft pine-covered ground just outside our stone hut, each with one eye open, alert, watching over us as we sleep. They guard the borders that, for them, define this place. Coyote hunts nearby. We hear his triumph but we have drawn our boundary lines with certainty. He does not cross over. I like that he lives close by. His endurance lends fine spirit to my journey.

Each morning, I bathe standing naked on a flat rock cliff high above the river that slips through the canyon. I brush the dogs and Persephone until they gleam. I attend to worlds around me: to Cougar, who suns herself on a rocky slope across the canyon directly opposite our grooming site. We are familiar by now with one another. Her fresh pug prints and our prints grace the mud banks of the river.

My mind quiets in this place of healing, enough that I begin to see. While morning shadows turn to light, I watch a wolf spider traverse the length of this flat boulder, this space we share. Her back is covered with babies, a rowdy bunch that tumble about, perfect tiny replicas of their mother. Another morning, a different type of spider walks across my path. Casually she slips out of her skeleton and walks on, a larger version of herself.

Spider wears her skeleton on the outside. Did you know that? When her skeleton grows too tight she steps out and walks away. Her bones remain, carrying her ancient story, a story written in Earth time. I understand now why Spider, according to mythology, promises emergence.

Across the canyon, an eagle nests in a jagged snag on a cliff, another neighbor in this place of great healing. I study her from my stone hut. She glows golden. Like the great Buddha she is, she holds inside the mysterious knowledge of light. Goldfinches fly between trees, singing as they swoop. Chickadees, their song unmistakable, socialize back and forth. Trim gray-and-white juncos scratch the ground for weed and grass seeds. Rough-legged hawks hunt at twilight. Raven — her brothers, sisters, daughters, and cousins — scratch their wisdom on my dreams.

Each morning, while I write, a raven preens above me
in a glittering rock alcove. She appears at times as the Black
Madonna and I tell her so. Pink rambling roses, purple violets,
and white star flowers spill from crevices in the alcove where
she sits. Pine boughs shade her face. Nearby, a fiery sumac provides a lofty perch for her raven community — La Comunidad.
Raven is insistent that I catch her message.

May I walk with you? I ask into the stillness of this healing
place. May I walk with you? During the day, sheltered from the
wind, I sunbathe with my books on our grooming rock, in this
healing place. Once a week I drive twenty miles to buy food and
replenish the five-gallon water containers. In town I am invisible. I loiter in the grocery store, overwhelmed by commotion
and stuff. Sometimes I swing through McDonald's (I know, I
know) to pick up four plain burgers, treats for my dogs. I stop
at the library for books and, later, read by candlelight.

We bed down early. Night slips softly into our small
hut. Stars drop by. The bright moon appears over a high ridge
beyond the pine forest. I never sleep the night. I wake to wild
song. Wild song in moonlight.

Can you imagine the music here in this world so large?
Wind passes through, carrying the scent of pine. My coyote
neighbors whoop it up. Spruce, Cedar and Oak whisper among
themselves. Bear splashes for trout in the river below where
Cougar drinks her fill.

A mysterious munching sounds from feathery pine
branches just above my down bed. Could it be opportunistic
Raccoon, the one who loves dog food?

I am never frightened here, but the night after the day I
watched a handsome king snake slither into his den, I worried

some. Then I thought, *Oh forget it*. After all, we are both animate bundles of chemicals common to all living things: carbon, hydrogen, oxygen, nitrogen, sulfur and phosphorus, different forms of earth dreaming—dreaming the song of wild things in moonlight in this healing place.

One night I dream a woman wearing a deep-blue velvet gown etched with lace. She is surrounded by clusters of stars. A raven perches on her shoulder. Raven wears a red gypsy cape and sparkly beads. She carries a golden coin under one wing. The woman walks beside me. "Be mindful of all who approach," she says. "How do you want to be?" Her words echo as Tibetan bells, "How do you want to be?"

I contemplate Grandmother Spider, how gracefully she shed her skeleton. I wonder if, like Spider, we are instinctually coded to step out of a too-tight skin. Could I leave my bones where they lay and walk on fresh and new? I close my eyes and imagine my bones on a rocky ledge.

Like Spider I walk on.

...onward full tilt we go, pitched and wrecked
and absurdly resolute, driven in spite of everything
to make good on a new shore.
To be hopeful, to embrace one possibility
after another — that is surely the basic instinct...

BARBARA KINGSOLVER
High Tide in Tucson

Walk On

Come along! A tumbleweed rolls by followed by the wind. "Come along," he calls. Off we roll. Soon we are stuck in a wire fence. We hang out for awhile contemplating life. "Life," he tells me, "is taking a chance." We blow off the fence in time to join a small band of tumbleweeds rolling into the sunrise. We roll or stay still. We are alive to touch the world.

One evening we are camped near a great herd of elk. The sunset is everything purple. "It is all yours," Tumbleweed says, calmly picking sand out of his brambles.

* * *

A pilgrimage has no rules. A pilgrim trudging along may stay on a safe and sane route following well-traveled paths to sacred sites. Another may climb a mountain to dance in solitude on edges, leaving behind tattered pages of poetry thrown to the winds. Another may explore his own heart in ways that pull him beyond boundaries to bedrock, to the place of wonder, indescribable in words. Yet another pilgrim may explore his backyard, exposing old patterns, issues, thoughts…shaking off ghosts, to grow into the blessed space of a larger world.

* * *

A woman walks the muddy banks of the San Juan river. She fishes a smooth round river rock from the water. Its strong slow pulse sounds in her blood. Earth and Spirit sound in her blood. Slow down. Listen. Listen for the song of the deepening breath. Once again she has come to this place, this back-to-beginning place. The place of the sweet small river Buddha, born out of earth and water and fire, caressed by water, rocked by water and eons of time.

How do I move? she asks. Asking to find the pieces of herself. She asks to breathe the broken, fragmented pieces of herself, her deities and demons, all one. A mosaic in the making. A movement made up of broken pieces. Awkward, unsure, not quite knowing…how to place the pieces. Or should she let them fall where they will? Unsure, she moves to come alive, to dig down deep inside to find what she has banished into darkness. She has come to this place daring to be vulnerable, not quite knowing. In a time of too much hurry she has come to the place of this sweet round river Buddha. This one who carries the seeds of the universe.

* * *

Breaking open. Picking up the pieces. Letting go all intentions of discovery…each walk has its own time, each step moves toward an unknown, a turn in the road, a willingness to stop for a while, a willingness to walk on.

Born of Water

Winged Grace

In the place where I grew up, our backyard rolled downhill through a dense wood to the shores of the Red River. The Red travels north into Canada, crossing the international border at Emerson, Manitoba, eventually draining into Lake Winnipeg. The waters of Lake Winnipeg join the Nelson River, which ultimately flows into the Hudson Bay Watershed.

In the misty light of morning, I followed the water's path along its muddy shore, where signs of nocturnal creatures were fresh. I imagined the lives of wild ones who made their moonlit journeys to drink from the river. I knelt to push my handprint into the gravelly mud, setting my track next to Sandhill Crane, Great Blue Heron, Fox and Badger, Raccoon and Snake.

Would the wild ones who met each night at the water's edge chance upon my mark? I wondered. Would they wonder about me?

Outside of town, down by the river, fog rose from the dunes where the river disappeared around a bend. Each curve pulled me deeper into the distance. I longed to walk on forever. The quiet adventure of a river walk, mysterious and cool, seeped into my bones like water smoothing over rocks.

One morning, at first light, I came upon a flock of sandhill cranes asleep in the shallows; their graceful silhouettes seemed as ethereal as the drifting mist rising out of the river. I remember feeling a tenderness, a stillness, an opening to the old slow pulse of things. I remember reaching down to touch the water as sunrise swept a blush of pink over the trees.

Suddenly wings filled the air. Groups of cranes lifted out of the shallows to perform their sunrise ritual, calling, swirling, circling. Breathing deep I ran, leaping forward, to dance on the cracked mud of the river's shore. Pulled into a place without boundaries I spread my wings following a map in my blood, a memory so ancient I dropped layers of thought to mingle with my sky brethren, in the red gray skies of dawn.

My ancestors honored the natural world, the blessed "Thou." My Scandinavian ancestors relied on devotion to a terrestrial intelligence to carry them forward. A great tree, the tree of life, dominated the center of my forebears' world. Ritual, theater, symbols and tradition opened pathways, spirit lines to a larger world. Long after the Christian church had been established — long after the Christian church had extinguished the old religion — artists and storytellers honored, in secret, Earth's teachings, embracing the sacred in all life.

My Swedish paternal grandmother, Emma, was a storyteller. My grandparents immigrated to America in the late 1800s, Grandmother from Sweden, Grandfather from Norway. They met and married in North Dakota. My grandfather died long before I was born. Grandma was an early activist — "Always

going to women's meetings," my dad would say. In one of
my early memories, Grandma and I are together in her
old-fashioned kitchen. I remember a screened porch off the
kitchen, blue curtains on the windows, and a rather sway-
backed linoleum floor. She is wearing a filmy dress that flows
just above her ankles, a fancy wide-brimmed hat decorated
with large colorful silk flowers, brown silk stockings, and black
heels with a cross-strap. Her dark hair curls around her face.
She has dark eyes and a very distinctive nose. Her voice is low,
a deep whisper, as though she is telling secrets.

She stirs the contents of several huge kettles bubbling on
the wood-fired cookstove. I sit nearby on a tall wooden stool.
She waves a large blue enameled stirring spoon in the air as
she talks. Fascinated, I listen. She is telling stories of the old
country — stories filled with fearsome ogres who hide under
bridges, intent on snatching an unwary child. Stories of dancing gypsies, lit by firelight, camped on the edge of town near
the dark woods. Stories of witches who live in the Black Forest,
witches who growl hoarse curses if someone ventures too close.
Stories of oak groves where townspeople go to worship. Stories
of warning and comfort and prophecy.

I am four years old and carried by her words to a legacy
of old ways. My grandmother was a teacher of the best kind,
a sanctuary where the rich and joyful colors of my heart could
bloom, a kindred spirit who fashioned wings for my soul.

*Nights used to be so much quieter
when Coyote sang.*

STEVE SANFIELD

Spirit Lines

When I travel, I carry rune stones to remind me of my ancestral ground. I also carry a beaded pouch, a talisman from my childhood, a gift from my grandmother. Inside: a cardinal feather, bits of bone, buffalo fur, an owl's downy feather, an elk pellet, a smooth black stone, a small pinecone, a tiny skull, a ruby ring, a North Dakota wild rose, a branch of sage. Each crackles with energy. This evening before bed, I choose the rune stone Ansuz, the messenger Loki, ancient trickster. Expect the unexpected.

While I sleep, lilting song rocks my cabin: Owl's haunting call, Coyote's ecstatic hoot. Eyes of the night watch over me. A night hawk perches on the bedpost. Sharp scents of sage, sun-drenched mountain pine, rain-swept hills, humid earth awaken all corners of my bedroom. Walls disintegrate. In my dreams, great herds of elk and buffalo race over unfenced land and through dark glittering skies. At the rise of a hill, shadowed by clouds and moonlight, a woman throws cornmeal to the stars. Wind, stirred by Elk and Buffalo's pounding hooves, carries healing streams of golden corn over the land and into my heart.

Sunrise. I open the door of the small cabin where I am staying. Dawn light radiates deep rose, orange, violet. I hike the mesa above my cabin, walking through radiant streams of color. Velvet air bathes my skin soft, ruffles my feathers, tips my fur golden, deepens my eyes wild. A howling pulses in my belly. My throat opens. Joyful howls and yips and bloodcurdling howls call me home to New Mexico's rolling hills, North Dakota's golden prairies, Minnesota's pine forests, Colorado's snowcapped mountains, Arizona's deserts, Utah's canyon land. Coyote's ground. Where spirits ride the wind and tawny laughter ripples on waves of tangy air.

Coyote's Ground

Each time I travel this way I am reminded of Earth's sensual nature. Female country. The realm of the shape-shifter. Transformation. All animals know about this.

The lodge sleeps, shades drawn, guests and management snuggled in. Bathed in silver moonlight, the surroundings seem suspended in time. I step out of my jeep, stretch and breathe air scented with sage. Yes. Nothing rushed. This is the time to see what is happening. This is the time Tarantula takes her outing. This is the time Coyote sings. This is the time Eagle flies to the far side of the moon, where in silver blue light Bear swims a deep wide lake and later grooms his golden coat on the sandy shore, while Eagle feeds her young bits of rabbit, fresh and warm. This is the time Rattlesnake dreams his mating dance.

Yes. Time to see what is happening. All animals know about this.

Two women stroll by. We whisper greetings. Is anyone around? I ask.

A night watchman checks me in, hands me a key to the bathhouse. Ahhhh! There, in the bathhouse, I shed my clothes. Steam rises. Heat seeps into my bones.

Later, much later, dressed for the night in flannel and fleece, I walk to my cabin. I feel catlike — all-seeing, quiet, secretive. The bright night is crystal cold by now. A handsome shaggy dog with amber eyes waits by my truck. He watches while I tote my gear into the cabin. He listens attentively to my musings while I unpack. He joins me on the porch for a long cool drink. Companionably we enjoy the late night's tempo. "This is the time," he whispers and throws me a wink. With a grin and a wag of tail he vanishes into the night, a trickster with red bells on his collar. His mischievous grin recalls mythic Loki, the arch-wise guy of Norse mythology.

I settle into my cabin and offer a prayer for this place of sanctuary. Tomorrow I will wake to New Mexico's rich autumn, to golden cottonwoods gracing the banks of the Río Ojo. Tomorrow I'll hike the high mesa, October's hot sun bleaching my bones white. But tonight, I am embraced by moon's fluid light. Wrapped in her ageless wisdom, I dream a world brimming with Earth's stories. Moonlight, a hint of sage, the scent of rain-drenched earth, and the music of hundreds of tiny bells fill my dreams.

Earth, sky and river flow in my veins.

In the distant hills, Coyote calls.

Setting My Track on Sensuous Ground

On a river trail early this morning, Coyote crossed my path. We both paused. Sunlight dazzled. Coyote glowed. I called out to her. She danced off toward the shelter of the bosque, fluid as waves of grass. She turned once to look in my direction then disappeared into the rich mosaic of gigantic cottonwood trees, graceful willow and fresh young sprouts; a grand bosque, spacious and healthy, fed by a free-flowing river. "Come howl with me," Coyote hooted once from the shadows.

I, however, caught in thought, plod along the river path and soon forget her…

"Come with me," River splashes, sending up sparkles. "Dance with me, float with me to faraway places beyond the mysterious unknown to the place where tens of thousands of grizzly bear mothers birth their young in a landscape of great care. Let's dance by the light of the moon leaving our prints on muddy shores in praise."

"Come with me," River calls as she rolls on by.

"If there is magic on Earth, it lives in water," Loren Eiseley writes.

We moderns have forgotten…

In early days, homage was paid to water. Divinities of water, the water gods, often appear at the beginning of a mythology.

Before birth we live in a protective film of water. The spiraling forms of our muscles and bones bear witness to Earth's network of water veins. Lines of flow on the surface of our bones can be followed right into the spongy bone structure.

We moderns have forgotten — *we are born of water* — fluid as a living river, fluid as silk. If rigidity has seduced your lovely sensuous self, be aware. Remember who you are.

"Come with me," River calls.

I throw my thoughts to the wind and follow River's elegant meander, all swirls and waves and curves. Sensuous ground.

My prints grow intricate and playful in the sand near Coyote's timeless track. Coyote's spirit part mine.

Last Night I Dreamed a River

Rivers and wolves, far-reaching horizons, migrating birds, and land give rootedness to my life. In this same place of grounding, in the pit of my stomach, lives a restless spirit. Perhaps it is instinctual, this restlessness. Archetypal. Something true. Perhaps we are as a species migratory, tribal as Wolf, fluid, meandering as a wild river, following age-old patterns. Our vision daring. Dazzling. Leaving only gentle reminders.

A step back in time? Oh wait, stop where you are. If truth be told, there is no time. All we have is the moment at hand. And that moment holds all that ever was, all that ever will be. A love story, transparent as the morning mist, if we let it be told.

In the early-morning hours there are candles for light, the ringing of a church bell and solitude. I follow a track upstream through Lavender Canyon. The heat of sandstone penetrates my bare skin. My rhythm changes to Earthbeat. Heartbeat. The place I want to be. I follow the track upstream to where wolves and birds, wind and water are the only sounds. Across the roaring river, a pair of osprey nest. I imagine the river coursing through their bodies. Lifeblood.

* * *

Today I walk where the river bends and flows north on its way to Canada. The river is frozen…several feet deep. Crystals of ice form on the shore. Thin patches of shore ice crackle beneath my feet. I crouch to sit on my heels. I break off a bit of crystal, hold it to my eyes. Rainbows flicker in the air. Light shimmers and dances over the ice. I test the ice with a jump, glide across the rough surface. I rest on my back. An angel in the snow. A pair of ravens fly close overhead, calling. The river flows beneath the ice, beneath my body.

* * *

Last night I dreamed a zillion stars fell to ground, and packs of dire wolves called up the moon. Last night I dreamed a saber-toothed tiger calling for his mate. Last night I dreamed a river flowed dark and cold and fast, carrying reflections of pine forests, whooping cranes and stars. Last night I dreamed I walked the shoreline along the river, a small figure in the face of all this greatness. I dreamed calls of migrating cranes rolling across night skies — I wondered at the intelligence in their bodies as they flew toward life-renewing marshes to rest and feed and dance. Each great soul gliding feet first, touching down in the shallow wetlands, calling to relocate family, settling in for the night.

I wake slowly from my dream. Have I taken a step back to a time when wildness ruled? That holy place in my mind where whooping cranes follow their flyways home? Oh wait, remember time, with her Cheshire-cat grin. Remember time,

supple as mercury, spirals and turns and swirls and bends.
Time, that illusive landscape where borders are fluid not fixed,
and Earth dreams.

Last night I dreamed a river dreaming her silvery dreams
of wildness...

Wildness...

*In my bones is the land itself. In
my blood is the river. In my cells,
the voice of the ancestors. In my
soul the dream of the earth.*

Territory

I know a woman born on the Northern Plains. At the
moment of birth, she drew the breath of golden eagle
down into her lungs. At the moment of birth, she drew the
breath of Hawk, Prairie Hen, Fox and Coyote. She drew the
breath of wild lands down into her lungs. Before her first step,
she understood that animals can speak. She understood that
the land has a voice. The land has her voice.

I grew up listening to the brush dance of wheat fields
in autumn, before harvest. Grasshoppers tuning up in fields of
grain. Raven's squawk, his swish of blue-black wings beating
overhead. The slow deep beat of frog song bellowing off the
distant pond at the edge of a dark wood.

When I was a child I freewheeled country roads on my one-speed Zenith, exploring the golden prairies out beyond town; or, on foot I forged a path through a thick tangle of woods and underbrush to reach the muddy banks of the Red River. There, the summer I turned ten, I buried my heart in ceremony one moonlit night; forever linked to rivers and wild silence, to the austere blue depth of far-reaching horizons, the freedom to roam. I hold dear to my heart and to my life this hallowed place.

I remember the smell of rich black earth held in my hands like a prayer, the angel-wing touch of a snowflake on my tongue, stately cottonwoods sheltering the old cemetery north of town, autumn leaves crackling beneath my feet. Crickets singing on a moonlit eve.

I grew up in a time when hundreds of antelope raced across the golden plains and the call of thousands of migrating cranes rocketed across the skies. I grew up in a time when endless waves of prairie grass flowed toward the far blue horizon, when the whistling wind echoing over the cliff edge carried mystery. I grew up in a time when a symphony of a different knowing crossed my everyday path — turtles and frogs, raptors, elk and deer and owl, coyote, cougar, nighthawks, bats…and fireflies.

Where have the fireflies gone?

Our world was so rich. Summer evenings my brother and I would slip out a bedroom window onto the porch roof overlooking our backyard. We watched the wondrous flickering light of hundreds of fireflies floating above the dark grass. Stars touched down out of the darkest sky, surrounding us. I called this place on the porch roof "the between place." Let's go to the between place, I would say. We sat there on the porch roof, a small space between two luminous worlds.

I lived on the Northern Plains, where once buffalo ruled the land and great migrations darkened the sky…

"As I look back on the part of the mystery which is my own life, my own fable, what I am most aware of is that we receive more than we can ever give; we receive it from the past, on which we draw every breath…"

EDWIN MUIR
An Autobiography

At the River's Edge

One year for my birthday, I received the published diary of Opal Whiteley, *The Singing Creek Where the Willows Grow.* That evening I flipped through the pages, intending a quick glance. It was well past midnight before I slipped this rare book under my pillow, turned off the bedside lamp, and fell asleep to the haunting music of Opal's words.

On the inside front cover of Opal's diary, my friend had inscribed, "This book is for the fine old spirit that rattles your bones."

* * *

I was four years old when we moved from Northern Minnesota to a small North Dakota river town. My baby brother, my mother and I arrived by train at night. My dad met us at the train station. We walked a dark alley to the house he had bought for us. Mom carried my brother. Dad held my hand and carried our luggage. In order to buy into the bank in this small farming community, he had sold our car.

* * *

"A fey child," my Mom says fondly. "You are such a strange little thing." What does she mean? I wonder.

We live at the river's edge. On gray winter afternoons, I walk the frozen shore. I wear a wool snowsuit, red knee-high snow boots, a knit hat pulled down to my eyebrows. The tip of my nose peeks through a fleece scarf covering the lower half of my face. I plunge through snow that comes up to my knees. Fog rolls across ground. Great old oaks and cottonwoods snap and groan. Flocks of small brown winter birds forage seeds and dried berries; they rise out of the brush with a roaring flurry when I walk by, scaring me. All around, I see signs of those who live here: a scarlet feather, a small pile of fur, a spot of blood, a splash of urine, fresh scat. Delicate tracks crisscross the perfect white snow. When I walk here, at the river's edge, the civilized world seems quite distant. Here, the world feels real, "all put together."

At the heart of our small town, a steel drawbridge spans the river. Heavy mist clouds the town center by the time I climb the icy dirt bank below the bridge and turn toward home.

This is my favorite kind of day, an aura of adventure held in the stillness.

"What did you see today?" Mother asks when we sit down to dinner. I describe my ramblings, but I do not have the words to say what I feel when I am out there in the woods down by the river.

Each autumn and spring, vast flocks of migrating birds — Canada geese, sandhill cranes, whooping cranes, raptors, black-birds — darken the skies, pull us outdoors to stand in wonder at the perfection of their formations, the power of their wings.

How do they know to do this? I ask. Mother explains patterns of migration, how instinct guides birds, as well as other animals. She explains instinct as memory, a genetic code, carried in their bodies from their ancestors.

She explains how animals and birds are drawn to energy fields in specific watersheds they have followed for generations. The land and the rivers and lakes are part of their family, she tells me.

When I am asleep, I dream layers of feathers warm my body. I dream wings.

* * *

My mother grew up on a farm. When we drive to the farm to visit her parents Mom and Dad drop my brother and me off at the corner, where four gravel roads meet and the woods begin. "Tell Grandma and Grandpa the kids didn't come," we giggle.

A shallow river curves through groves of oak, elm and cottonwood, circles a twisted tangle of brush and fallen logs, meanders past an apple orchard. In every season, the apple orchard is a magical place. In the spring, craggy old branches hold fragrant blossoms. My brother and I walk side by side beneath the branches. I imagine we are in a secret palace garden.

I imagine this is a place where wishes come true. Summer trees are heavy with apples. Little green worms hang from tree branches swinging on thin strands of silk. My brother and I loiter, toss apples, play hide and seek. Then, in a flash, we are off running, racing to see who will "beat" to the farmyard. "Surprise. Surprise!" we holler. Our grandparents, waiting on the steps of the back porch, oooh and ahh as though astounded by our arrival.

I stand near the locked gate in the barnyard to greet the grand old bull, Mick, who lowers his head, paws the ground and snorts from a far corner in his arena, avoiding me. I throw crusts of bread, intended for Mick, to a line of ducks as they parade by headed for the duck pond. I visit each stall in the barn where a newborn colt or calf or baby goat may rest on fresh hay. I tiptoe into the chicken coop knowing not to disturb the plump nesting hens. Carefully, I reach under each one to search out a warm brown egg to bring to Grandma.

* * *

If we are lucky, our parents plan a visit during branding season. Branding season is neighboring time. Trucks hauling horse trailers pull in to park helter-skelter on the gravel drive. Men head for the corrals. Children scatter. Women carry platters of food into the kitchen. Grandma's kitchen, always a hubbub of activity, becomes a whirlwind of laughter and hugs and cooking. Mouthwatering smells drift from open windows—baked ham, fried chicken, biscuits, gravy, mashed potatoes, sweet corn, beets, cakes, pies. Picnic tables scrubbed and covered in red-checked oilcloth await the feast.

Meanwhile, dust billows from the cattle pens down by the barn. Lanky men on horseback separate calves from the herd.

The calves, rounded up and held in corrals, kick their heels in the air and bawl piteously for their mothers. Nervous mamas mill around on the other side of the pens, calling for their babies. The branding iron sizzles. Admonished to stay out of the way, my brother and I, and a pack of other kids, hang out at the corral. Like a line of crows we perch on the top rail of the wooden fence. A cowboy skillfully whistles a rope through the air, aimed toward a hapless calf. Cowhands wrestle the resistant calf to the ground. Zap! It's over in an instant. All blood and dust and confusion. We cheer the calf as he leaps from the ground, throws his feet in the air, and scampers off sporting my grandpa's Double E brand.

I remember the noise, the dust, the commotion, the sizzle of the branding iron, and my grandpa's assurances. "This did not hurt the calves."

Life on a farm revolves around seasons and the work that must be done. The household wakes before the crack of dawn to tend to chores — the care of animals, fields, barn, machines, house and people. By afternoon it's siesta time. I climb the narrow wooden ladder to the hayloft, where I dream the afternoon away, read, or simply gaze out the wide double doorway. I imagine how it would really feel to leap from the hayloft into the golden haystack on the ground below. My uncles did this when they were boys. They tell of the utter joy of the leap. My mother hushes them with "the look." The look has a voice of its own: "Don't give her any ideas."

I stand poised on the sharp edge of the wide opening, leaning out to earth and sky. The distance seems deep, the haystack below very small. I picture myself swirling into the air, slow motion, feet pedaling, skirt billowing, hair lifted around my face.

When I visit the machine shed, I pull myself up to sit high above the ground on the steel seat of a tractor. I imagine driving the great tractors and combines, eating lunch from a black lunch bucket, in the fields, with the men.

Everything on the farm fills a purpose: the root cellar where Grandma stores garden vegetables, the great Clydesdale horses who pull wagons filled with hay, the cattle, the grand old bull Mick, dogs, chickens, cats, roosters.

* * *

Grandpa and I walk to the barn, at dusk, carrying clean steel milk pails. Grandpa pulls up a short three-legged stool for me. I sit next to him while he milks his cows. Sweet faced cows glance over their shoulders, mooing softly. A tiny calf sleeps in a nest of hay. I wait patiently until Grandpa asks, "Would you give me a hand?" It takes a lot of my strength to squeeze a stream of milk into the waiting pail. Twilight filters through dusty windows, a diffused golden light forever mingled in my memory with the smell of warm milk, fresh-turned hay, and soft murmurs of contentment. The last thing Grandpa does before we leave the barn is set a pan of warm milk on the floor for the barn cats.

Later, in the milk house, I watch Grandma churn butter, separating the fat from the milk. How smart she is, I think. "Who taught you how to do this?" I ask.

My grandparents are bound in a special relationship to this land. My great grandfather's brother Benny immigrated from Sweden in the late 1880s. He laid claim to several sections of rich North Dakota farmland through the Homestead Act by living in a cave on the land for a year. Grandpa's farm, and the adjoining farm, grew out of Benny's perseverance.

My great grandpa farms the land next door. His house is three stories high with white gingerbread trim along the roof line. A screened wraparound porch gives the house a grand feel. Oak, cottonwood and willow trees shade the flagstone walkways. An adobe barn crouches in the distance. My uncle lives there, too, with his wife and my cousins. Everyone is always busy at the house, around the barn, in the gardens. People are everywhere. The children seem alien in their coveralls and straw farm hats. I am not comfortable with them. And although I think the place is very beautiful, I don't feel free to roam, as I do at my grandparent's farm.

A majestic nickel-plated wood-burning cookstove dominates the kitchen in my grandparent's rambling farmhouse; the pantry smells of ginger. Before dinner, Grandma and I walk down a sturdy wooden staircase to the cool stone-walled basement. In the fruit cellar, tall wooden shelves hold rows of clear glass jars filled with homemade canned goods — plump purple plums, red beets, tiny orange carrots, small yellow corn cobs, green beans, apple sauce, cucumber pickles. The jars shine like jewels.

Every autumn, Mom and I spend a day at the farm during canning season. By the time we arrive, Grandma and the aunts are at work in the steamy kitchen. Apples, plums, apricots, picked that day, and vegetables fresh from the garden soak in steel tubs on the floor near the sink. An assembly line of sorts forms spontaneously. One person washes, another peels, another fills sturdy glass Mason jars. The jars are set in frames to boil in huge enamel kettles on the cookstove.

During canning season, my job is to fill baskets with vegetables from the garden, haul the baskets in a wagon to the back porch, sit down on the steps, chop off the leaves, throw the leaves in a barrel on one side of the steps, then toss the vegetables into large steel tubs on the other side of the steps.

I pull carrots from the ground and smooth away the rich black earth. I gather armfuls of beets, prickly cucumbers, green beans, peas, rutabagas. While I work in the garden on these hot, humid autumn days I send up prayers that someday I, too, will marry a farmer.

At the end of the hallway on the second floor is "the girls' room," the bedroom my mom shared with her two sisters. Flowered wallpaper, faded and cracked in places, covers the walls. A pitched ceiling, papered in lilacs, gives the room an impish shape. White goose-down pillows and comforters piled high on narrow cots hold a whiff of lavender. When we stay over, I sleep in this room.

An arched doorway opens onto a rooftop balcony. The scuffed floor of the balcony is painted tar paper over plywood. Over the years the tar paper has buckled and softened. I walk onto the balcony with the sensation of walking on a cloud. A white banister encircles the balcony. From where I stand, leaning over the banister, distance stretches on forever. Haystacks shimmer gold in the fields. The smell of fresh-turned earth drifts in the air. As far as I can see, puffy white clouds float in blue skies. The silvery river melts into the horizon. A green John Deere tractor parked by the barn looks like a child's toy. A wooden rain barrel set beside the back porch takes on the look of a hunched black bear. A pair of butterflies, cornflower blue, attend to a tuft of free-spirited daisies near the outhouse.

In the hallway, just outside the girls' room, a pull-down ladder leads to the attic, where hats of all shapes hang from hooks on the walls — old straw farm hats, wide-brimmed frilly hats, velvet hats fitted close to the head, feathered hats, felt cowboy hats. Worn work boots, patent-leather church shoes, cowboy boots, fancy open-toed heels line the floor along the walls. Gaily decorated trunks with brass fittings are packed with filmy camisoles, fringed dresses, fur capes, beaded purses, embroidered velvet slippers, sparkly scarves: treasures my Grandma, Mom and her sisters have carefully folded away. I spend hours in the attic playing dress-up, inventing stories to go with each outfit.

My grandparents' bedroom is furnished with massive dark-wood furniture. Inlaid dragons and gargoyles snarl from headboards, cabinets and dresser drawers. I know from stories told by my grandmother that this furniture came from Ireland, where her ancestors still live. In the corner of the bedroom, near the closet, a full-length, freestanding, gilt-edged mirror catches the gargoyles' reflections. The gargoyles seem to move and dance about as the light changes.

I covet the brass gargoyle bookends on my grandfather's oak roll-top desk and hope he will give them to me. "Grandpa, can I have these when they get old?"

"Gargoyles aren't for children," he answers. "Let's find something else to think about." He reaches to the top shelf of his bookcase for a game of marbles. I covet those marbles, too.

The children in my hometown are warned each winter never to play on the frozen river. We know sure as nighttime falls, powerful currents flow beneath the ice, dangerous whirlpools, deathly cold water.

My fifth-grade classmate Keith drowned during spring thaw. He slipped off an ice floe in his effort to help a dog struggling to get its footing among the huge chunks of floating ice.

The boys with Keith screamed for help. The town sirens blew, signaling tragedy. Everyone ran toward the river, each person's face gray with fear, eyes alert, staring straight ahead. Each heart hopeful. My dad and Keith's dad happened to be together as they ran toward the river. Keith's father said, "I know it can't be my boy."

Today, when I remember Keith's death, I remember a town in mourning for a young boy. We, his classmates, sat together in the Methodist church where his services were held. For most of us children, this was our first funeral. Our grief was private. We came to say good-bye to our friend, a boy with sparkling eyes and a broad smile; a boy with chestnut hair, whose chubby cheeks were covered in freckles; a gentle, kind boy. Keith Steinbach.

* * *

During the school year, when classes break for lunch, I hurry downtown to meet my dad and our spaniel Lazy, who naps under Dad's desk at the bank. We walk the few blocks home together. I match my steps to my dad's and I learn to walk very fast. Sometimes I skip to catch up. He never slows his pace.

After school, my best friend Ruthie and I stop by the bank to ask Dad for a couple of nickels. Pocketing our coins, we trot across the street to the drugstore, climb up onto tall ice-cream stools, lean our elbows on the marble counter and order two Dickies; a Dickie is an exotic concoction of vanilla ice cream topped with chocolate and marshmallow sauce, served in a fancy glass sundae dish and eaten with a long-handled silver spoon. More often than not, my five-year-old brother shows up at the drugstore. How does he know when to find us? We snub him with our superior girlish ways. However, we admire his unique way with money. He looks up at the fellow behind the counter, extends his empty palm: "Ice cream, please," he offers politely. In moments he receives a strawberry cone.

* * *

On winter weekends, the kids in town converge on the outdoor skating rink. We skate until numb toes force us off the ice into the warming house. Wood smoke hangs in air pungent with scorched wool. We crowd together on sturdy wooden benches to pull off our skates, then stretch our sock-covered feet as close to the wood-burning stove as we dare. Too late for some of us. Some of us cry while we slowly, slowly unlace our skates, unable to bear the pain of frozen toes, finally freed. Some of us cry all the way home. There are days I simply hobble home wearing my skates. My tears freeze to my cheeks while I pray fervently for Mom to be home to warm my feet in her hands.

During the summer, we play baseball in backyards. We argue with our friends, call names. More than once, the town bully chases me home. One day, too far away to reach home, I race into a neighbor's yard to hide. Too late. He's right behind me. I run up the porch steps and bang on the front door, wailing for help. He has me cornered. I curl down on the top step. He runs up close, pounds a fist in my face, and scurries off. Blood pours from my nose. This is the same nasty bully who shot my cat with a BB gun. Bobby Evenson.

Down the street from my house a swamp flourishes. Morning glories bloom, tadpoles grow tiny little arms and legs and vanish into the frog world. Fresh-faced turtles sunbathe on half submerged logs, slip off to swim, to burrow in rich mud.

This swampy haven — home to blackbirds, hummingbirds, wading birds, shorebirds, bumblebees, mosquitoes and flies — carries the calls, chirps, hums and buzzes of creatures possessed by the richness of a muggy wild place. The fragrance of loamy soil, tiny plants, velvet-tipped flowers and dewy grasses saturates the air. Hundreds of frogs sing from their lily-pad thrones, crickets chorus their pleasure, dragonflies dance. At night, unseen nocturnal forces shriek, performing rituals of mating, birth, death.

One afternoon, my brother slipped off the bank into the swamp, the sticky mud at the bottom sucked at his feet. He struggled. I could not reach him. Terrified, I turned toward home screaming for my mother. I see her still, running full out, down the gravel street, toward us, alerted by radar a parent taps into when their child is in danger. She wades in, grabs my brother out of the swamp, clutches him close and carries him home. I trail behind. The blackest of mud and tendrils of slimy green stuff drip from the two of them as though they are one. I imagine a smelly swamp monster waddling down the road. I giggle to myself, barely able to contain a hoot of hysterical laughter. Not long after this, the swamp was drained.

* * *

My girlfriends and I spend hours in my playhouse trying on party dresses and makeup from the costume trunk. We outfit ourselves and my brother in wide-brimmed hats, long dresses, heels; we add lipstick and rouge to our baby faces. Our next step is to parade around town. We buy candy cigarettes in the dime store, sit on red-leather stools at the lunch counter, order chocolate sodas, and smoke.

* * *

At the back of our yard, across from the garden, is my reading tree. I carry books and snacks up into the high branches. I write poems there, too. Some poetry I tear up and sprinkle in the air. Some I save; later I bury the pages in the cemetery. For my expedition to the cemetery I pack a peanut-butter sandwich, Oreos, an apple, my poetry and a few comics. I place all of this and a jug of water in my bicycle basket and pedal the mile or so out of town.

A graceful black wrought-iron fence circles the grounds of the cemetery. I park my bike on the dirt trail near the entrance and walk through the stately gates. Wildflowers bloom, the grass is high, unkempt. Prairie winds brush over the grasses creating a shushing sound like a river. Angels, cherubs, lambs, the Virgin Mary and various saints decorate ornate marble tombstones. I stop by each tombstone to read elegant engraved remembrances. I place my poems under stones and clumps of dirt. Would the spirits find their gifts? I wonder. I settle in my favorite place, under a grove of cottonwoods at the edge of the cemetery, to watch for ghostly bodies who like to read poetry. I eat lunch and read comics. All around the perimeter of the cemetery, craggy cottonwoods rattle their sparky old tunes.

* * *

Just before our Eskimo winters freeze the river solid, my dad readies his workshop. He cuts a cord of wood from the forest below our house. We stack the wood on the porch outside the shop. I await these preparations with great anticipation. I love the shop — the mysterious array of tools, the crackling warmth from the potbellied stove in the corner, the intermingling smells of burning wood, linseed oil, turpentine, varnish, sawdust. This is Dad's territory. Here too, I have the feeling of a place "all put together."

My dad always has a project on hand for me. While we work, refinishing the beautiful antique furniture he loves, I listen to his rumbly voice call up the "olden days." Before long, the shop overflows with people and events from another era. Omar, Dad's beloved older brother, who died at the age of five from diphtheria, finds safe haven in this small space, as does Abe, a younger brother. Abe was an Air Force lieutenant in World War II. His plane, the Burma Bitch, was shot out of the sky. Neither Abe nor his crew were recovered.

My grandmother received an invitation to the White House, where, in quiet ceremony, she accepted the Purple Heart, awarded Abe's family in return for his life.

Releasing the Wild Heart
of a Nomadic Woman

"By the roots of my hair some god got hold of me.
I sizzled in his blue volts like a desert prophet."

SYLVIA PLATH

At the Crossroads

O ur marriage. We eloped. We phoned our shocked parents. We honeymooned. It was "the holidays." We returned from our honeymoon to spend Christmas with my parents. We were welcomed as a married couple. It was done.

My husband, a blue-eyed dark-haired Irishman, was all a woman could want: devoted, responsible, handsome. In love with me.

We set up our household in the university town where I was writing my dissertation and my husband was completing his final year of law school. Within a month, I knew I did not want marriage. This had nothing to do with him. My father's words returned to haunt me.

"You are not ready for marriage. Be your own woman first."

How do I get out of this? Tentatively, I brought my concerns to my parents. They were astonished, unsympathetic. My new and loving husband was devastated when I cried, I want out.

Within two months of our marriage, I was pregnant. This was the daughter I knew in my heart. The night she was born, my husband and I talked all night — so amazed by our baby.

Her wise baby face, familiar in my dreams, carried the wisdom of an old soul. Two years later, our handsome son was born. We adored our babies. I was a wonderful mother, a terrible mother.

My internal struggle with marriage lasted ten years. Finally I could be there no longer and took measures to leave. Divorce, especially initiated by a woman, was almost unknown. I had no model for this. I had no good reason. Our friends, our families, did not understand.

The marriage looked good. Why? Why? What was wrong with me? Our children were crushed. We were all in free fall. To many, and ultimately to myself, I abdicated my most primal responsibility.

We struggled for balance.

Our friends were no longer my friends. The person I was no longer existed. I returned to the university to continue my studies. My children and I moved into university housing. The dynamics of our lives changed greatly. I found a young boyfriend. I was sensitive, insensitive. My mistakes were thousandfold. I wore guilt like a shroud.

In a dream, I climb to the top of a pyramid too steep to be comfortable. I find a beach where I lay in the sun on white sand near the water. A shark comes by and swallows me whole.

Immersed in fear I pace the length inside the shark. I feel his heartbeat. His breathing carries the sound of bells. I call his name. Shark dissolves. I walk on the beach with a friend. It is nighttime. The sand sparkles. I reach down and pick up a small, very fine diamond. As I hold this diamond in the palm of my hand it grows to become a glittering crystal ball. I throw the crystal ball to my friend. We do this back and forth in play.

A cluster of stars streaks across the sky falling to ground. My footprints grow deep, tracing star patterns in the sand.

Marie-Louise Von Franz writes in *The Way of the Dream* of following your star as accepting isolation, not knowing where to go, having to find a completely new way for yourself instead of just going on the trodden path.

So the caravan is on its way.
I can hear the merry gypsies play.

Van Morrison

Releasing the Wild Heart
of a Nomadic Woman

For a time chaos takes my hand and I stand at the edge of the abyss where everything falls apart.

I dream a gypsy woman. She breaks through a crumbling wall of cement and walks toward me. I feel I am her baby. She picks me up as a husk. She breathes life into my body.

As an alchemist of old, Gypsy stokes the furnace. She breathes her child, my body.

Breathing woman to life.

Gypsy carries a feminine wisdom eons of years old. Of Sophia, Shakti, Kali, Tara. Disintegration. Wielding the sword of discrimination. Renewal.

Spinning the wheel of time, Gypsy breathes my woman to life. She breathes my form for this earth walk, at the edge of creation, where earth and spirit meet. Fire. The red six-teen-spoked wheel in the center of the gypsy flag recognizes Gypsy's East Indian origins. Legend weaves images of gypsy mystique. Rich colorful traveling caravans. Prophecy and song. Grave dark-eyed children. Firelight. Shadowy dancing figures.

Gypsy sister walk with me, for I am on a journey to a sacred place. To accept the gifts of soul. Wheels of time moving me.

Waking to a shower of gold.

Remember we are granted one moment at a time…to dance across earth with passion, suppleness, and simplicity…as wind, water, and sand…as something magical.

We leave a legacy of trails across the land, a legacy of spirals and sage, crushed grass, green and blue waterways, as we move through time, lovely and mysterious.

Everything comes to us at last.

If we let it be so.

It is very soothing to know this.

"Know yourself," Gypsy reminds.

Following Gypsy's invisible tracks I walk a path into the far reaches of my soul, spiraling deep, smashing through years (lifetimes) of holding back, hiding her, devaluing her. I walk the labyrinth of time throwing open narrow corridors of thought, throwing out pretension and emotional detachment. I crush scorn and self-righteousness, stomp arrogance. I turn away all lies of success breaking though rusted old barriers of judgment. I walk away from betrayal and denial. I dare to uncover the demeaning critic living dark and cold and men-acing behind my heart. I face grief, allowing long-held tears to flow. I face difficult experiences and barbs from time past. I accept my anger.

Following Gypsy's invisible tracks, I walk toward passion. Passion, the catapult into the unknown. I dream pristine prints traced deep on the rain-washed shore of a wide blue mountain lake. I dream a raucous chorus of hoots and howls and yips from Coyote's silver-coated clan camouflaged in a stand of willows on the shore of the lake. From the center of the pack Ed Abbey's voice rings loud and clear. "The human-centered view of the world is anti-Christian, anti-Buddhist, anti-nature, anti-life, and anti-human!"

Viva Abbey! Viva Coyote! I shout into the star-filled night.

I hunker down under my bedcovers holding on to dreamland. "Stay true. Stay true," the silver-coated throng hoots. Gypsy dances in the light of the full moon.

The extreme clarity of the desert light is equaled by the extreme individualization of desert life-forms.

ED ABBEY
Desert Solitaire

Women on the Road

Certain writers have touched my soul over the years — John Nichols, Terry Tempest Williams, Barbara Kingsolver, Linda Hogan, Mary Sojourner, Joseph Campbell, Carl Jung. Doug Peacock, Rick Bass, Frank Waters, Peggy Pond Church, Sally Carrighar, Tony Hillerman, Barry Lopez. Thomas Berry — the list goes on.

It was Ed Abbey's *Desert Solitaire* that first opened my eyes to time beyond the scope of conventional boundaries. His playful, loving, erotic, deeply felt sensibility toward Earth and her creatures, his despair over careless attitudes, his true irreverence, grabbed my bones and sent me reeling into the heart of the Southwest.

I have traveled far — where roads are empty and haunting, hot sun seeps into my pores, and the shimmering light has an energy of its own. Desert country's eroded shapes, dusty soil, and endless skies touch a genetic code.

Wind whips over the land, dreaming rattlesnake and sage. Wind clears my mind, opens my animal heart. We dance, Wind and I. Wind twirls Dust. Dust Devil twirls, swooshes, and disappears. Hey, just disappears. I turn all around. Dust Devil returns, catching me in his embrace. We dance on sunbaked ground. My skirt lifts. My hair swirls. We dance to a desert beat, Dust Devil and I. We whirl and twirl. Towering buttes, deep arroyos, short twisted sage shimmy and shake. Sheens of brilliant light ripple over the desert floor. Puffy cloud people waltz overhead. Graceful willow sway. I shout. I am home! Wind catches my words. "Home," Wind whispers, gentle as a breeze.

Those of us who have fallen in love with the desert Southwest know how it is. A land timelessly dreaming. When I drop into this place in my body, a larger wisdom draws me into the mystery. I lose myself. I step through gateways to dream with Earth. I walk with rogue spirits to learn the meaning of intimacy. If you, too, hike or camp alone, as I have learned to love, you listen for the coo of a mourning dove. A canyon wren's cascading song draws you to a blue fire stream flowing through a canyon slit. Thin as Snake you sidestep, your chest scrapes rock, you slither and slink your way through cool darkness to another time. A sharp-eyed, earless leopard lizard, at home on a narrow crevice, attends your passage. The slot opens to layers of jumbled red rock. A baby rattlesnake curls in the shadow of a spindly sage. You step aside.

On a warm summer evening, scarlet skies spread over the land, deepen to indigo, darken to jet black, glitter with star constellations. If you are lucky, you may catch *Datura* opening her white trumpet flower to the night sky. Once you are sound asleep, the hunting cry of a screech owl, the death cry of a tiny desert mouse, may break through your dreams. Dazed you sit up to peer through the tent flap. You crawl outside, stretch and listen. Perched in a tall cottonwood near the stream, Owl silently tears his mouse to bits. Far off, maybe twenty miles, or fifty, from a place where Gila Monster buries her eggs in July, thunder booms. The cool desert ground beneath your bare feet shivers in anticipation. Wind rushes over rocky ridges, ripples through moonlit canyons, rattling the tops of trees. If you listen, you will hear rain dreaming that far-off place where Gila Monster young emerge from Earth's deep heart.

Dark sandstone canyons curve and turn narrow. You walk a floor of slickrock down to a steep red-walled gorge; small footholds in the face of the rock entice you to climb to a hanging ledge, where ancient ruins keep their secrets. In the distance, a haze of rugged shapes shimmer — cobalt blue, purple. A rainstorm blows over in a minute and you revel in the scent of sage. You stand in the middle of everything and look off to forever. Coyote lives here. He makes his home near sandstone fins; he rests where naked shale and clay crevices give cover; he hunts where prehistoric ruins crumble and turn to ground. Coyote roams hidden grottos, he drinks from deep blue pools, he races under waterfalls. He jumps frogs who burrow in cool sand under moss-lined creek beds. Cougar lives here. Vulture, Spider, Bobcat, Lizard, Fox, Eagle, Rabbit, Snake, Rodent, live here — and so the desert breathes.

Tough-shelled insects live here. Dung Beetle lives here. Tiny critters who seem huge when they crawl across your sleeping bag. Gambel's quail, the little fellow with the teardrop-shaped topknot, lives here. Noisy blue Scrub Jay nests in piñon and juniper. All live and work here. It has always been like this.

Medicine plants live here. If you are graceful, if you are grateful — if you know how to be with them — they offer their secrets. When you understand how to be in the desert, you will have the power to change the way you live.

My daughter Kelly, our dog Frosty and I travel together. It is late August. We leave Denver without map or fixed itinerary. We carry borrowed camping gear and a cooler filled with food. Just at sunset, we take a left turn off I-70 onto 191. A small brown sign points to the right. We start down a narrow rugged road.

Cliffs loom on both sides, darkness closes in around us. We bump along for a while — stilled, uneasy. I realize I am barely breathing. Finally I turn to Kelly. What do you think, maybe too remote? My voice shakes a little. Kelly agrees. I turn around and head back to 191. We swing back onto the dark road as though alone on the planet.

I pull into the parking lot outside the closed visitor's center at Arches National Monument. A map of Arches posted on an information board lists a campground. An arrow on the map points to a campground at the end of a curving road. From where we stand, I see a strip of winding blacktop snaking up the side of a steep canyon wall. Stars, then a full moon, appear in the dark sky. Moonlight and land merge. I drive slowly, climbing up and up. Bathed in cool blue light and immense space, we seem to be floating.

Huge rock shapes grow out of the far distance. Time slows. I drive on through a moonlit landscape, our car a dark silhouette, a small spaceship cruising alone.

We roll into a campground at the end of the road, the only visitors. We set up our tent, crawl into our sleeping bags, relieved to be someplace. I wake to a misty morning. A luxurious silence. We seem to be at the top of the world. All sky and distance. I set a breakfast of bagels and hot chocolate on the picnic table. Kelly rummages through her camera bag. My eyes feel soft as silk. We mosey along a red-dirt path. A vast red-boned land opens before us. We are quiet, chatter seems out of place, our voices too loud. I brush against a sprig of flowering sage. I reach to break a twig, to crush a leaf between my fingers. Instantly I sense her life and pull back my hand, remembering. Remembering a more natural mind.

I catch a glimpse of Kelly just up the trail. She looks a part of the land, no bigger than a blade of grass. She is beautiful. I hunker down in the cradle of a great sandstone arch. Earth slips into my bones, my soul grows exuberant.

Two afternoons later we travel back down the curving road. Mist hangs over the horizon. The hint of blessed rain.

In Moab we restock the cooler at a market on Main Street, eat lunch in a small café. I marvel at the exceptional taste of my eggs and bacon. I realize my senses have sharpened, my rhythm has slowed. After breakfast we visit the shops. Kelly replenishes her film supply. Already, I grow tired with the scurry of people. Although Moab is a small town, the noise of visitors, the push, the eagerness, are overwhelming. I feel my eyes grow hard, my breath shallow.

Soon we are back on the road. West of Blanding, we venture off the two-lane blacktop onto an old jeep trail. A dusty faded track meanders over the desert floor, curling around juniper, piñon and sage. We follow this mellow sunlit trail and disappear into the dream of the desert. The light parts and bends around the jeep. The scent of ripe juniper berries tinges the air. Our path takes us to an abandoned corral shaded by a giant cottonwood. I pull to a stop near an empty water tank. A windmill whirls slowly in the breeze.

Kelly tugs out her camera. She leaps out of the jeep. Autumn leaves from years past layer the ground where she stands. Light dances in hot sun. This land is alive with a vibrant energy I have never known. A shiver runs down my spine. I feel as though I have arrived at the beginning of time. Kelly straps on her camera bag. We walk along a shallow ravine. The ravine opens onto a slickrock plateau dotted with clear pools of water ringed by sandy beaches crisscrossed with fresh animal tracks. I kick off my shoes and sit with my feet hanging over the edge of a deep pool. Kelly strips down, dives in. Our little dog, Frosty, who normally avoids even a puddle, hops into one of the pools. I lean back, sinking into waves of heated stone. The shimmering light shifts. I close my eyes; my pulse slows, merging with light and earth. I place my hands on my belly to touch Earth's ancient story.

Eventually we walk on, slide down a rough salmon-colored cliff to catch the ravine. Frosty's damp white fur turns pink. Kelly is smudged with earth; we wear the colors of the land. We follow a lazy shallow blue stream entering a lush oasis of thick rice grass, tamarisk thickets, brush and cottonwoods.

We can go no further. High above, sheltered in the shade of a slickrock shelf, a stone ruin dreams. I imagine shadowed forms moving about on the ledge, at home. A hint of woodsmoke drifts on the air.

We reach Natural Bridges National Monument late in the afternoon. This beautiful place is alive with the history of former residents. The three natural bridges bear Hopi Indian names: Sipapu, Kachina and Owachomo. A sense of the prehistoric remains; a feeling of such remoteness, I would not be surprised to see a giant cave bear feeding beneath one of the great stone spans.

Again, we are the only visitors. Intrigued by lustrous faces and dancing figures emerging from rock walls, I comment to a park ranger. Desert varnish, he tells us, and explains how minute amounts of iron and manganese mix with particles of soil on damp rock-wall surfaces. Over time, a thin dark veneer builds up; rainfall crafts the ever-changing patterns. Yes, yes, I nod, pleased. My mind loves this information, but my heart leaps to embrace the teachings of my grandmother. I remember the old ones, *Dísir*, spirit guardians of the land.

From the ranger, we hear about a prehistoric culture, people who once occupied the Natural Bridges area and the larger region of the Four Corners. They appear to have vanished mysteriously, walking away from cooking fires, leaving pottery and tools in place as though they intended to return. I recall the tranquil cliff home we saw yesterday high above ground, protected from visitors. Perhaps they did not leave, I think.

One evening I settle near a canyon pool to write in my journal. A mountain lion arrives for his evening drink — so silent, so beautiful. I freeze for the moment before he notices me and bounds off. There are no words to describe my feelings or impressions. We do not have a language large enough or pure enough to describe his power and grace, his compelling presence — the presence of a being totally at home in his body, at home on his ground.

Kelly and I break camp the next morning. We are caught up in giggles; the joy of it all bubbles up, uncontained. Weak from laughter, giddy, we toss our gear in the jeep and drive off for parts unknown. I pull off the road at a place that shall remain unnamed. Here, we dance on edges. Geologically. Physically. Emotionally. In holy blessed joy.

We gaze out over space, over desert, river and rock formations, hundreds of feet below. Hours later, we return to the two-lane blacktop. I cruise — not at breakneck speed, but we are sailing along, not a care, lighthearted. Wham! Screech! I brake wildly, my breath stops.

The jeep skids to a shuddering stop. We have come to rest perched over the same view we had just been marveling at, only this time our jeep's two front wheels are pointed directly over a steep drop-off. Steep, a thousand feet steep! I look at Kelly. She is pale as a ghost. "How could this road just end?" To our left is a sort of dugout hugging the side of a cliff. When we step out of the jeep we see this dugout rolls almost straight down. "Is that a road?" I ask. We ponder the situation. We take time to recover. Shall we head down this road-that-is-not-a-road, or turn around and circle back the way we came? We decide to take our chances on - the - road.

I am stiff with tension when at last we touch down on a respectable two-lane blacktop. I stop the jeep, jump out and kiss the solid desert floor. I need a walk. We grab our packs to follow a worn sheep trail. Pillars of black volcanic rock shimmer in waves of heat. I lean into the ruby heat of an ancient rock face, feel her slow pulse rumble through my body.

We pitch our tent in a primitive campground on the shores of the San Juan River a few miles outside a small desert town. In the last light of the day a glowing rise of cliffs beckon. We climb into a world alive with petroglyphs.

I wake to a mellow whisper of voices. When I open the tent flap, I see a couple of "river rats" just a few feet away, readying their kayak for a float. Does the town have a restaurant? I ask hopefully. Thumbs up! Ahh yes! Let's go. I give Kelly a little shake. We are starved. We treat ourselves to a scrumptious breakfast and a morning's exploration. I love it here. The little town seems charmed.

We strike off to drive more rough roads. Kelly photographs desert horizons sweeping on forever: a hardy Mesquite protecting Roadrunner's brushy nest, sunset backlighting a windmill's dark silhouette. She shouts, "Halt!" leaps out of the jeep, trots off into a ditch, or field, or cliff, crouches on the dusty earth and waits for just the right light for her perfect shot. Late in the day, we travel a particularly twisty gravel road across Navajo country. Blood-red evening skies turn dark. Gradually zillions of glittering stars appear surrounding the jeep.

We are oddly untroubled by the fact that we are lost. Since we had no destination, it seems irrelevant. Kelly suggests I continue to follow the old green truck clanking along ahead of us. "He looks like he knows where he's going." Far into the night, we drive. At last, surprisingly, we arrive at a campground. I hop out of the jeep, dazzled by stars, the immense distance. I stretch into the glittering atmosphere.

"Where are we?" I ask the ranger who appears out of the night.

He laughs, tells us we could have cruised these roads all night. "The roads out here are tricky, unmarked, branching off in all directions."

Wading through stars we set up our tent. I want to sleep outside but what about snakes? I end up sleeping on one of the picnic tables. Early the next morning, Kelly, Frosty, and I hike a dry riverbed to faraway ruins. We wend our way over rock and up ridges; we squeeze through tight crevices following a sort of trail. This is the same trail where some years later I will step on a sleeping rattlesnake. Before we leave, we visit the tiny visitor center of this faraway place. The ranger suggests we visit a special canyon on this last lap of our journey before returning to Denver.

He draws a map on a torn piece of newsprint. He sketches a few short squiggles, one long line, a dart where a field of silver sage bunch up. "Turn left at the sage clump, continue straight at the sunflower patch," he says. He places the sign of a leaf. "Or is it right?" he muses scratching his head. "Oh well, you'll know," he grins. He draws in a square at the top of a hill to signify a trading post. "If the blue door is closed, he's open for business. Stop for further directions." The ranger nods, satisfied. "Although he's rarely open," he mutters to himself. He hands me the map with a grand gesture. We shake hands. I thank him for the map and stuff it in my pocket.

A rough gravel road snakes through a lush canyon. Native stone farmhouses with dark-blue-tile roofs nestle, comfortably old, with the land bordered by green fields, peach orchards, red-rock walls. I pull over to park at the edge of an arroyo. I walk to the top of a hill overlooking grassland meadows, wild-flowers. I look to white-sand canyons where scaled, feathered and furred critters live. I look to stately cottonwoods gracing the banks of a wide ravine. My shirt snaps in the wind. My hair twists around my face. My heart cracks open. A raven squawks. A black feather tinged with purple drifts past the jeep's door.

"Carry that into your dreams," Kelly laughs. Hmmmm. I imagine Raven's place in my body. How would that be? Hair will grow straight, and dark. Talons will be sharp, eyes will glitter with far sight. Flight will be swooping, strong, playful. In time bones will whiten on desert ground.

Stories will be told.

I return again and again to the desert's vast heart, sometimes with friends or family, most often alone with my dogs. I love the anonymity, the blessed space, the sheen of light dancing just at the corner of vision. I return to make my home in small southwestern communities, places where I am close to desert, mountain and river. Committing to what is significant to me, something in myself I do not fully understand, an energy that pulls me so strongly I cannot resist.

Every Footprint a Song

On the Prowl

An hour after daybreak mist drifts over short-grass plains. The road I travel curves around Northern New Mexico's rounded hills, through forested valleys where emerald-green ferns flourish. I drive past quiet adobe villages, where candles cast a glow in dark windows.

The road I follow winds upward toward rocky peaks crossing a snowy pass cut into the mountains. Clouds of mist conjure memories of another place, where a young girl roamed — images of thriving wetlands and deep stream-fed lakes scattered throughout a northwoods forest, home to Owl, Eagle, Hawk, Wood Duck, Loon, Elk, Heron, Frog, Turtle, Trout, Water Snake, Wolf. A place where a young girl paddled a wooden dinghy through cattails and sedge grass, far out into the dark center of a somber lake, and dropped anchor near a small island. Steep cliffs rose from the water, rough and blazing white. Golden eagles claimed this territory, emerging out of dense gray fog, coasting low, casting for trout.

* * *

I enjoy the invisibility, the slow-motion feel of a misty day, the air of mystery. Borders between worlds vanish. My cluttered mind gleefully leaps into the glowing coals of my animal heart.

I dream the exotic jaguar, who disappeared from the Southwest years ago.

Recently, a lone jaguar was sighted in the Malpai Borderland, a high-plateau badlands along the Mexico border in southern New Mexico and Arizona. In the early 1900s, jaguar were hunted as predators and for their beautiful fur. By the 1960s, breeding populations had disappeared from the United States. Jaguar are listed as endangered in North America. Endangered from Mexico through Central and South America.

Jaguar was once the most powerful cat in the Western Hemisphere. Wrapped in her golden coat with its distinctive indigo rosettes, she graced the realm of Mystic. Pre-Columbian rituals honored Jaguar as Goddess. Throughout Central America, Jaguar inhabited the fine territory of myth. Her presence on earth enlarged life. Jaguar images found their way into sculpture, tapestry and history, celebrating her power and beauty.

Our modern world, fragmented, troubled and overpopulated, infused with the hubris of the human species, lacks a sense of the sacred, or wholeness. In the case of Jaguar, as with many vital creatures, we have turned centuries of respect into hatred and death. Loss of territory, death for fashion, slaughter for its own sake have successfully eliminated the jaguar from this industrialized country.

If this unlikely sighting be true, I consider her presence a miracle. She has crossed dangerous borders. I have no illusions of seeing her, nor do I really want to. I simply want to offer a thumbs up for the territory she inhabits. A salute to the fact that, so far, the human species has failed in its attempts to exterminate another incredible animal.

* * *

On the outskirts of Santa Fe I choose the scenic route; destination Socorro for the night. However, when I stop for gas in Cedar Crest, I find myself in conversation with a volunteer for Hawk Watch. She is on her way to the Manzano Mountains, where she will join other volunteers in the migratory bird count. They will also be releasing several rehabilitated birds to the wild. The gathering site is Capilla Peak — at 9,200 feet, a vantage point in the Manzano Mountains, high above the tiny village of Manzano.

Manzano, an old Spanish village, holds an energy all its own. Very private. I do not linger. I travel upward on a rocky potholed gravel road to the crest of Capilla Peak. Thousands of sharp-beaked raptors sail the thermals. The holy migration of raptors! Eagle, Redtail, Swainson's Hawk, Kestrel, Falcon. All fill the sky with sound and wing, close up and personal.

I park my vehicle in a small campground and walk toward a cluster of people. Winged breezes singe my hair with electricity. The young volunteer I spoke with earlier prepares a rehabilitated kestrel for release. She asks if I would like to do the honors. I don a pair of leather gloves; the little hawk hops onto my outstretched finger. He is still attached by a cord on his ankle. He is so alert. I know he smells freedom. His rapid heartbeat matches my own. His whole being stretches toward the sky. I unhook the cord. He pumps his wings to join in flight with all his fellows.

Firelight melts across the sky as I drive toward Socorro; hot red colors — tangy orange, magenta, a dash of red pepper, a touch of cinnamon, a splash of lemon. I meander along a peaceful stretch of road, winding through a wide canyon. The rhythm of the road lulls me into reverie. I recall Bruce Chatwin's beautiful book, *Songlines:* ode to the Australian Aboriginal who walked his songline to honor his lineage. His songline represented himself, his family of origin, his ancestors, his way of being at home on this earth. I imagine the little kestrel soaring, his sharp eyes reflecting firelight. Winging his songline home.

I skirt Socorro and drive on toward Magdalena. Just beyond Magdalena I notice a B&B sign. Usually I avoid B&Bs because they don't allow dogs, but it's almost dark and I'm tired. We'll check it out I tell the pups. I pull off the black-top onto a dirt drive ambling through half a mile of sage to a brightly lit ranch house.

The Rancho Magdalena is a working ranch. Longhorn cattle, horses, goats, free-range chickens live here. Our hosts, Lee and Lori, welcome us. A bunkhouse along the courtyard side of the ranch house has been renovated to accommodate guests. My delight knows no bounds. My bed is piled high with pillows and a white down comforter. A kiva burns in one corner. Maggie and Hopi Girl settle on soft rugs scattered over glowing tile floors. A window faces the back pasture, where a herd of horses graze. The last rosy light of sunset fills the room.

We are awakened way too early by a group of range chickens who peer in the sliding glass door of our room. Maggie and Hopi Girl are shocked by this. They give me the wide-eyed look, ears set back in concern. I give them an "it's okay" grunt and fall back to sleep.

I dream a jaguar prowling through a tall grass prairie, prowling a high rocky ridge, prowling a maze of red-rock canyon — Jaguar on the prowl.

Dreaming Tracks

L avender rays of late-afternoon light dance over canyon walls. Nighthawks swoop and play in darkening skies. Stony mountains rise in the distance. A great gray owl disappears into the forest. The wide river murmurs her dreaming tracks across the land. Outdoor springs steam and bubble. I step into the water and sink into bliss. I imagine myself fluid as the river, sultry as the evening air, invisible as a fox.

* * *

Tall lodgepole pines conceal all but the tin roofs of abandoned cabins on the opposite shore of the river. A broken-down bridge — planks jutting up, side rails collapsing — entices me to cross. My dog Frosty and I slow-step over rickety rotten boards. River splashes up.

Wildflowers bloom, untrammeled. A path winds through a grove of Arizona cypress to a small log cabin. I push open the door. A wonderful square oak table sits in the center of the kitchen. A stone fireplace fills one wall, the wooden mantel holds a dusty copper pot. The spacious, tranquil, sunlit room invites me to stop awhile. I sit down on a sturdy wooden chair pulled up near the oak table. Pine boughs brush against worn window screens. Soft breezes ruffle faded blue curtains. A bay window overlooks the lively river. A family of mice peek up at me from a cracked floorboard. What happened here? I ask into the silence.

* * *

It is dark when I set up camp. The night air carries sounds of a sea long gone. A silver moon glides above high rock walls, casting her cold glow over the land. Great old stone faces appear. Sea creatures rest here, great bodies, faces, fossils, fins, preserved in rock and soil. Ah yes, I whisper, I know you. And in the night while I sleep, Sea washes over me, tumbles me, dreams me awake. "Listen." Sea sounds. "Listen for the steady voice of River. Listen for birdsong. Listen for the deepening breath of your dreaming. Listen. Listen for music drifting across the edges of blue canyons. Listen for the Ancestors. Listen for the song of Love. Listen.

Morning light filters through the open flap of my tent. I poke my face out to a wilderness of rose walls etched with a patina of mahogany. On a grassy knoll, not twenty feet away, a small band of horses stand quietly eyeing my tent, chestnut coats aglow.

My dog barks. Silently they slip away.

I follow a faint trail along the ridge of a canyon, gradually weaving my way downward. Hoofprints guide my way. A clear shallow stream flows over white sand on the floor of the canyon. A small herd of horses dream in the shade of pink rock walls. A flowering orchard catches my eye, so unexpected I stop and stare; I take a few steps in that direction. I notice a small home and gardens, a Navajo woman hanging clothes on a line. I realize this canyon is home to Navajo, not just here for my hiking pleasure. This is their land. I turn to walk in the other direction.

* * *

Frosty and I walk a gravel road. I carry our lunch, a canteen of water, and my camera in a day pack. Soon we are joined by a friendly black-and-white dog. Wherever we walk, a symphony of bells echoes a melody so subtle I wonder if I am imagining this sweet harmony. Could it be the light, pure air producing this sound?

A Navajo family pulls up in a truck and stops. A woman calls out, "Do you want a ride?" No thanks, I say, but what is that sound of bells? "Our sheep," they tell me laughing. We wave, they drive on. Later, I do see sheep and goats munching grass on a very green hillside. I notice they are spread out all over the hills blending beautifully into the landscape. Hundreds of sheep and goats. All wearing bells.

At dusk I return to my vehicle and drive toward the highway, my mind caught up in images of the people and their homes, dusty roads vanishing behind red-walled mesas reappearing far off; sandstone pedestals, pinnacles and mesas a reminder…of Earth time.

Unconsciously, I take a right turn onto the highway. My plan was to travel in the direction of a small town nearby, where I'd intended to spend the night. Once I realize I have turned in the opposite direction, I am afraid to turn around. Darkness covers the land. The edges of the road blend into the landscape. I fear I may go off an edge into the depths of the void.

Mysterious outcroppings, so compelling in daylight, now take on an ominous look; fins, like gigantic sharks, loom out of the darkness. I remember this is ocean floor. Seabed. Time has morphed, boundaries collapsed. For all I know I could be traveling under the sea.

The road is empty of traffic. No comforting lights of civilization. No moon or stars light my way. No landmarks signal familiar ground. I talk to Frosty, who sits alert and watchful on the front seat beside me. By now I am scrunched down in my seat, my head pulled into my neck like a turtle. I peer through the top half of the steering wheel mumbling a chant of sorts. At some point I hear Frosty say a word, a word resembling Hello.

So, she speaks our language now, I think. This does not surprise me and lifts my spirits somewhat. I talk on hoping to hear another word. Nothing. Not a peep.

In the darkest of dark distances, I think I see a flash of light. I'm sure. My attention transfers to thoughts of civilization. Lights are sparkling in the distance! The road spirals steeply downward to a narrow bridge spanning a dense dark abyss. The abyss seems to rise menacingly to grasp at the edges of the bridge. I close my eyes until they are just slits and point the jeep straight across. I am desperate to reach the other side, where the welcoming lights beckon. A restaurant/bar/motel hangs over the gorge, barely connected to land by a contorted spindly structure of two-by-fours. Where are we?

In the morning, we prowl the town, my fluffy white dog and I. We stand on the edge of the abyss overlooking the river far below. Blue skies roll on forever. My blood runs hot for this vast space of sky and land, generates an excitement for more of the unknown. Instead of turning back, I decide to drive on.

A narrow highway curves into the land. Red cliffs cradle the river, sighing the breath of Great Grandfather Time. Great, Great, Great Grandfather Time. Ahead, a fortress of jumbled magenta pinnacles and castles rise as far as I can see. I follow the road, a luminous serpent opening gateways.

Oil

Once upon a time, not long ago, I found this place, a place of deep serenity, where if I was quiet, respectful — if I took my time to be here — I could watch the spirits dance.

A crystal stream once flowed clear and lively along the floor of one of the side canyons here, a seep originating from a moss covered grotto below an ancient Pueblo where old ones dreamed, where they placed their mark on canyon walls offering blessings, where Cottonwood, Willow, Fern, small desert flowers, and berry bushes thrived.

This stream and the underground aquifer that birthed her has been polluted by oil drilling in the area since my first visit some years ago. The water, once clear and lively, lies dead, stagnant, covered in a glittering slimy sheen. What lived and spoke, what thrived for thousands of years, is gone.

Quality

On the street where I live the grandfathers' tread is firm and sure. The old men, their homes, and the fields below our houses shimmer above the plaza. Whenever I walk to their homes they are at work, repairing a roof, chopping wood, clearing a ditch, feeding their horses: Work essential to their body and spirit. They remind me of my father. They remind me of the long-ago cougar in Natural Bridges National Park. At home on their ground.

What is this quality? I ask my friend Amanda. Their stories cover so much ground: childhood, sheep camps, the Korean War, logging, children. Family. The quality is in their humor, the impish twinkle in their eyes, the gentleness of spirit, a straightforward savvy intelligence. Do you know the loss? I know it, too. This loss of quality in our lives? She understands, although I struggle with words.

We are hiking where the red willows grow, near the river, past Pilar. "It is the agrarian culture," she says. "People who live with the land. There is also in our culture a protocol of respect and manners." She whispers, almost to herself: "In the elders." We are quiet for a time. I wonder about this quality of protocol and respect. Where has it gone? This quality of self-assurance. Of humility.

Amanda's father grew up on a ranch in the mountains above Tres Piedras. As a child Amanda rode with her father and his brothers, herding sheep from the high country through the canyons to their sheep camps on the mesa. She hiked with her father, learning the ways of plants and animals. She is of the land. We both are.

"Paul had it," she says softly. "He was cut from the same cloth. Lately, I have been thinking of him. I see his walk, or a gesture, in someone else."

Eight years ago, Amanda's husband, Paul, died of a heart attack. A young man.

We continue our walk. We reminisce on the familiar memories of growing up on the shores of a river. Amanda finds a spot near the river to sketch. She pulls a pen and pad from her pack. Before she settles down she grins, dances a circle arms outstretched, exhilarated by the beauty of the day. She turns to face me, her expression exuberant. "To grow up on a river," she says, "the most primal place, always remembered."

I walk upstream along the muddy shore, the air fragrant in pine and moist earth. On the opposite shore in a grove of cottonwood, an osprey claims his territory. Black bear range further uphill, invisible to me, feeding on berries and grubs abundant this fall, building fat reserves necessary for hibernation. Mountain lion shelter in the hills above the river. Deer bones, scattered and stripped clean, give evidence of their presence. Graceful mud baskets built one beakful at a time, plastered to the underside of rocky ledges, are cradles for swallow babies, their parents' sweet lullaby a part of river's song. I walk to the summit of a craggy hill; limestone ledges command a fine view of río's meander and the faraway beyond. Osprey swings out from his snag, coasts over the sheen of water, sharp eyes alert for that wily trout who hangs out in a channel beneath a submerged log. Around the bend, a pack of coyotes set up their dusky calls. Calling out the wildness of home.

You coyotes know everything, I hoot.

Viva Coyote

I jog along the narrow street where I live toward the plaza. In Kit Carson Park, I take a few turns, pass through a gateway, to find myself in another world. A forest of flaming-gold cottonwood trees grace a dry arroyo for as far as I can see. On the banks of the arroyo I walk through a carpet of golden leaves. I am immersed in gold.

I follow a crooked animal track as one of the critters who lives here. No need to be seen. Here is the world my body knows, shadowy and sunlit. A world unseen until I take the time to be here.

Shy, but deadly, Rattlesnake curls under the rough bark of a sage bush. Rattlesnake rarely confronts. He offers a polite warning and will escape when possible. One summer day, while hiking a remote trail in Utah, I stepped on a small rattler. I rounded a bend and there he was. Too late to stop, my foot pressed down. He shot off into the brush. I hopped up and down in circles, shaking off the fear. That encounter still lives on the sole of my boots.

Tarantula—a large, handsome ground dweller—hides out during the day. She hunts at night. However, you may see the dark-brown male cruising during daylight hours intent on finding a mate. His daytime outings contribute to his short life-span. The cautious orange, black-striped female may live twenty years or more.

Other spiders who live here build intricate webs to capture insects. Spider has been around for millions of years. Some cultures revere Spider as Grandmother. Creator. Teacher.

Rodents, rabbits, insects live here, each contributing to Earth's balance. Bobcats, lizards live here. All creatures wary. Living by the laws of nature.

Black Bear moves through here. Seldom sighted, bears know that by "freezing" they can, in most cases, escape being seen. This year, a serious continuing drought, and human infringement on their territory, has forced bears closer and closer to the human world, the dangerous world. Coyote lives here. Lean and hardy, Coyote works the land with great spirit.

Early one morning in Yellowstone National Park I watched a pair of coyotes work as a team, walking in tandem, carrying a huge elk leg in their mouths to their pups. Later I watched the lone female protect her pups from a pack of three juvenile wolves, each wolf twice her weight. Her barking and yipping, her fierceness steered the wolves from her hillside den.

That afternoon, I watched her move her four pups, one at a time, to a new den. And still later at sunset I saw her and her partner strolling along the banks of the Yellowstone River. Four pups followed, romping, playing—attending to Mom's voice. Learning to hunt. Told when to hide, be silent.

God's dog, some call Coyote. Cunning and intelligent, she has managed to outlive, outlast, outwit many opponents.

Coyote thrives in the town where I live, on the streets where I live, in the houses, the gardens, the cafés, the courtyards, the shops. Coyote, a master of camouflage, tucks her tail under skirts and baggy trousers. She wears bangles, scarves, jeans. Cowboy hats. She drives trucks and jeeps. Passenger cars.

In a moment, Coyote can pull on the mask of invisibility. One minute you may be chatting with Jeanie, admiring her new beaded ankle bracelet, while standing in line at Cid's. You glance across the aisle to wave to Alberto. You turn, and Jeanie is gone. You may catch a glimpse of a golden brush of tail slipping around a corner, a golden leg, graced with a beaded ankle bracelet.

On a cold winter evening, I walk home after a delightful dinner at the Apple Tree. I cut across a field and trot down a snowy side street. I pass the house where my friend Eloy lives. A chorus of yips and howls drifts over the high adobe walls. Curious, I pause to push open the gate to peek into the courtyard. Yikes! A throng. A pack. A gaggle. Sipping margaritas. Talking politics. Telling jokes. Grinning. At least fifty coyotes dressed for the night, their thick furry coats adorned with sparkly scarves, beads, feathers.

Viva Coyote! I howl into the night.

Waiting at a stoplight on Salazar one morning, I glance over at a teenager sitting in his truck, gnawing on a power bar. He finishes his snack, takes a quick look in the rearview mirror, adjusts a few stray hairs with his paw. He notices I am watching, he flashes the old Coyote grin. The light turns green.

Descansos

I live on Valverde street in a lovely old adobe house within walking distance of Taos Plaza. I have settled here to write, or as one friend put it, "It is time you hunkered down in front of your computer to write a tribute to your wild heart."

The life of our street and the life of the plaza could be a hundred miles, or lifetimes, apart. We hold our breath, trying not to be discovered. Our street shimmers above the plaza. Daily life happens here. Leo walks his six-year-old granddaughter to school each day. We gather wood, haul wood, chop wood, clean the acequias. Horses and cattle graze in the fields behind our homes.

Coyotes yowl. Stories are told.

Our morning ritual starts at five. We step outside, sniff and check our borders. Fleeting shadows linger. Who has crossed from here to there? Stray dog? Cat? Coon? Coyote? Amber-eyed Bobcat? With grand deliberation, my dogs bolster their territorial claims. We return to the kitchen to start breakfast; the espresso machine hisses. I settle down to write. Morning hours fly. A friend phones. "Do you have time for a walk?" We walk through Kit Carson Park, follow an invisible track toward the hills above the Pueblo to watch eagles soar.

Later, I putter in my yard, visit with my neighbors, hear stories from a time ago. I walk to the library to spend a few hours with research. Afternoon sun warms white-washed adobe walls. Five o'clock: church bells chime. The fragrant scent of piñon draws me outdoors to walk narrow curved roads on a warm, still evening when snow falls fat and heavy.

A tradition lives on in New Mexico. A cross is placed at roadside sites where an accident has happened, or an individual has died; a cross, festooned with jewels, garlands of flowers, the blessed virgin, to mark where Angels kneel to pray. *Descansos.* Rest in peace.

Farewell.

Descansos for my friends, the animals. Farewell, rest in peace. I kneel to place a sparkly cross among the rocks that mark our newest grave.

For you, young Skye, baby kitten, roses for your generous spirit. A sage cross, high on a hill, marks your passage, Barney Boy, you fine old soul who nipped at the heels of Elk, and napped on satin pillows.

A cross of daffodils and aspen marks sun-spun Frosty's grave, my fearless laughing brown-eyed dog. A pine cross marks little Wally's site, pure love. A cross of stone and wildflowers for shy black cat Persephone. And for you, Lady, a cross with jewels.

Now, Max, my faithful friend, for you a cross of hearts and soft green grass. For Sadie, courageous mommy cat, a cross of red rock, white clouds and pink skies. For Maggie, the smartest girl on the block, a mandala of smooth river rocks and sprigs of four-leaf clover. And for you, my Hopi Girl, my golden girl, my soul mate, a cross of wildflowers and blue sky, mountain meadows and sage.

We found you, Goldie, under the trumpet vines, a calico kitten no bigger than the golden leaves falling from the big old cottonwood tree nearby. You were so beloved by us, your family, Charley and I, Catman and Siam. Your sweet self graced our home beyond all words. For too short a time.

Descansos for my parents.

A crane, inlaid in turquoise, marks your cross and life-times of love, Mom. Your dancing spirit still holds me safe, each day, lifting me to soar. Images come together in time. Images of grace.

July, the summer I turned eight, I woke out of a lazy dream to sunlight filling my bedroom. The house was quiet. Too quiet. Where is everyone? I rolled out of bed, looked out my bedroom window, over the porch roof, beyond the branch-es of the huge old climbing tree, across the alley to the garden. You stood at the edge of the garden, your arms raised to greet the rising sun. You wore a pale yellow dress. All around you, the world glowed, honeyed gold: the plants, the sky, the leaves on the trees. I ran down the steps and out the back door to be with you.

You were the lifeblood filling our home with warmth and beauty. Your strength of love was subtle, fierce, constant. At the time, I could not have said how important this was. Or even known it to be true. It has taken me long and hard, with deep-est sorrow of regret, to appreciate how generously you loved.

Thank you, dear heart. Garlands of flowers for you. Forever. "Farewell. Sleep well."

A cross for you, my father. Your sternness, your wit, your quirky mischievous grin. Your razor-sharp mind. Your gentle spirit. You were always yourself, never out to impress; yet you were so impressive. When we walked together I always tried to match my step with yours.

I carry in my heart teachings of love, always. Stories you shared that I may glimpse the depth of the man beyond my father. Your love for animals. Your morning wakeup yodel. Your focused attention. Hand-picked roses, in a crystal vase, on my bedside table. Cocktails in the kitchen before dinner. You and Mom together, sidekicks, shoulders touching, sharing stories of your day. This I hold in my heart, the love story you shared.

Not long after your funeral, you sent me two dreams. In the first dream, you and a group of your friends danced a line jig on a cabaret stage. Individually, you wore different hats. During the dance you exchanged hats. You were all grinning from ear to ear. In the second dream I was touring a house with a realtor. She pointed to a fake waterfall in the living room. You appeared, tapped me on the shoulder hard, and whispered, "I'll show you where the real spring is." You zipped down a dark stairway to the basement. I stood on the threshold, unsure. You returned and offered your hand. I followed. Seeking the real spring. The wellspring.

Love Forever.

Down to the river I go.
Walk down the gorge,
Something within the abyss
Waits for you in hiding. Go!

NANAO SAKAKI
Break the Mirror

Go

Some years ago my friend Jeannie drove Highway 68 for the first time. She rounded the high curve overlooking a wide valley where the Río Grande Gorge snakes across the plains to the north.

"What is that?" she gasped. She parked her car to the side of the road, got out, and stood at the edge. In the distance, the tiny village of Taos shimmered in the late-afternoon heat beneath the rough peaks of the Sangre de Cristo Range. Rounded hills, green with piñon, sage and pine border the western ridge of the valley. Volcanic rises dot the plains. The jagged mouth of the serpent splits the earth. She shivered under the hot August sun. *"Madre de Díos,"* she whispered, "could anything be more terrifying, or more beautiful?"

Deep in the belly of the gorge, seven hundred feet deep in places, runs the Río Grande. Birthed near Stony Pass in the San Juan Mountains of Colorado, once known as the El Río Bravo del Norte (Wild River of the North), the Río Grande, Our Lady, has been tamed, dammed, viciously violated. Her wild meander channeled.

* * *

A snowflake falls, touches ground, melts, seeps underground, flows downhill to pop up in a bubbly spring that flows further downhill to form brook or stream. Pure enough to drink, the life-giving stream joins the headwaters of the Río Grande. One thousand eight hundred and eighty-five miles later, Our Lady empties into the Gulf of Mexico poisoned by irrigation, garbage, chemicals, untreated sewage, and assorted floating objects. She is a living river no more.

Our Sacred Lady.

*Sandhill cranes drank the water of the Río Grande,
and ate the fishes, frogs and other water animals that lived
here, and they all lived well. Even though the sandhill cranes
did their very best to drink up all the water, they could not.
"This river must be very strong," the Pueblo people agreed,
"so here we will make our headquarters; here we will
build our nests and increase in number."*

PICURIS PUEBLO CHILDREN'S TALE

Down to the river. Walk down the gorge. Go! Deep in the gorge, outside of Taos, New Mexico, a wild river flows. I watch rainbow trout, flashes of iridescent green and silver, dart up from the deep cool river to grab a fly on the wing. I mosey along the river's rocky shore where black basalt cliffs tower, where hundreds of swallows swoop in acrobatic swirls, where red willow grow, and beaver build their homes. I notice the swallow's horno-shaped nests plastered side by side on cliff walls. I take my time here, where life moves to the rhythm of the river. I stop to listen for the river's voice.

I wait at sunset, when swallows by the hundreds fly home to settle for the night. I listen while they sing their babies to sleep, their sweet song a part of the river's song. I too, lulled by the song of the river, may slip into meditation, unencumbered by rules of meditation.

Sociable Raven notices when I arrive at the river. Suddenly ten or twenty gather, circling overhead, chatting. Praying for a death? Or a corn chip? Perhaps they think I am a catch. Whatever it is, Max, my faithful watchdog sits at my shoulder, jealously guarding, when Raven comes to call.

Ravens hold a special place in my heart. When I was a kid a neighbor nursed a baby raven fallen from his nest. He named him Charley. We all visited Charley and brought him treats. When Charley was old enough, he was released to live on his own. He nested close by. In the morning, before school, I would stand in our backyard with a treat on my shoulder, food or something sparkly. Usually Charley was waiting, perched on the edge of our garage roof, anticipating me.

When I whistled or called his name, he flew down from his perch, snagged his treat off my shoulder and carried his treasure to his nest.

In time Charley attracted a mate, who did not share his trust of humans. She convinced him to nest with her by the river in a grove of cottonwood. How do I know this? One day when walking the river trails I spotted Charley's nest. You may ask, "How did you know this was Charley's nest?" A sparkly trinket, wrapped around the base of the nest, caught my attention: a special gift I had offered one day, a gift of diamonds, or maybe it was rhinestones. Viva, Charley!

Rarely do I see "song dog." I bear the smell of danger. Human. However, one early morning, when hiking near the river, I top a rise. Just below me, on the sandy shore, a coyote pack rests, possibly twenty or more pups, a few adults. Max stands stunned for a moment, as do I. Then he barks, just one shrill bark. All heads turn. Coyotes lazily glance our way, amble to their feet as one, cross the river, golden fur aglow. Camouflaged by Red Willow they turn to face us. Still as can be, they watch until we leave.

Every Footprint a Song

"I live to walk," a lone stranger whispers to me as we pass one another on a trail outside of Taos early one morning. My soul goes giddy. So there are others.

Once a month or so, I drive the road to a nearby hot springs. I rent one of the cabins and spend a few days hiking the mesa. Life remains unbroken here. A primal presence remains deep in the land, a presence I can almost touch. This mesa is blessedly quiet. And the spirits love quiet.

A jeep trail meanders over the mesa through rounded hills and low rambling mountains toward far-distant small villages. The distance compels, seems magical, darkly beautiful. I long to walk the trail all the way to El Rito. I prepare my pack and study maps. My first night out, I camp in a blissfully beautiful meadow. I wake the next morning feeling disoriented, out of sorts. I pack up camp and start walking on what I remember is the trail. Before long I realize I am hopelessly lost. I wander for hours, trying to pick up the trail. By noon I feel panic setting in. Exhausted, I sit down; tears fall. I doze.

I dream the delicate ringing of bells. No, it *is* bells. I walk to the sound, toward a sheepherder who is moving his flock to another pasture. He suggests I return to the hot springs. He directs me to the right path. Near dusk, I hike off the mesa, walking the embers of a New Mexico sunset.

What I have discovered traveling New Mexico is to be still inside. Be still. I will find my way. Why is this so difficult? I forget it all the time. The fact is, New Mexico is all about letting go of notion, and importance, and expectation.

Let go. Be still.

On one of my early travels in New Mexico, I was lost on a two-lane dirt road I had followed into a maze of crumbling white cliffs and crooked old piñon. An enchanted bonsai garden, I thought. Bedazzled by the landscape, I drove on. Eventually I turned onto a gravel road that curved upward into a village. A huge double-storied adobe church fronted a dirt plaza. Small adobe homes lined three sides with a courtyard in the center. I parked my car in the shade of the church.

I saw no one. I walked a winding dirt road past small farms. Cattle, geese, donkeys, chickens moseyed toward the fence to check me out as I walked by. A few dogs ran to the road barking halfheartedly. Flowers bloomed in gardens, lusciously unkempt, tumbling over crumbling adobe walls — purple and white lilacs, deep red hollyhocks, blue morning glories, tiny purple violets. Masses of sweet peas.

Daisies grew wild. Apricot trees were heavy with fruit. A delicate scent of spice filled the air.

The road continued through the gates of a cemetery gloriously overgrown with prairie grasses, sage, a riot of wildflowers. Stately crosses, many dated centuries ago, bore Hispanic names.

Elaborate arrangements of flowers adorned each grave site. I paused to take it in. I had never seen a place so alive.

I rested here, in this place of beauty, in this place of renewal.

Gateways

The rumpled shapes of New Mexico's blue black hills open gateways to other dimensions, intimate landscapes where stories dream. Stories angle out of the rock rubble of copper, cinnabar, fire opal, turquoise. Stories whisper from rivers and streams, call out from the tips of golden cottonwoods. Stories are heard in the power of a raven's wings. Stories live in whitened bones scattered over the land; they touch your heart with their hunger to be heard. When you walk in the desert on a hot summer day, you may want to stop, kneel, listen to a story told by the smallest wildflower. A story of forever. A story of endurance.

* * *

I wake drenched in sweat, gasping with fear. I shiver as I try to shake off the nightmare. The clock on my desk glows red in the dark. It is just after midnight. I throw on jeans and a sweatshirt.

Now what was that all about? I ask myself. I turn on all the lights in all the rooms I pass through. In the kitchen,

I shake coffee beans into the grinder. The familiar ritual of brewing coffee calms me somewhat, yet I nervously pace the kitchen. The disturbing images of the dream are all too real.

I pull on boots, grab a jacket, pour a cup of coffee, and step outdoors to the small walled courtyard. I perch restlessly on a patio chair then jump up and set out into the night.

I hurry through the silent plaza. At the corner, I cross a dark street and walk the few blocks to a narrow gravel road. I follow the winding road until it turns into a barely visible two-track jeep trail. I jog through rough stands of winter-brown grass toward the sagebrush hills.

This is homeground, where I have spent years roaming the sweet meadows and rolling hills. I open my arms to embrace the star-strewn sky, the expansive landscape scented with sage, piñon and dusky earth. Primal ground. I place my palms upon my belly. I offer prayer to that wild place within. I turn. The eerie snow-white face of Taos Mountain glowers, massive and majestic.

In the distance, below the mountain, I glimpse the soft rounded curves of an old mud *morada* almost hidden by the surrounding hills. How long, I wonder, has it been since I have taken time to be here? I walk toward my old sanctuary. This particular prayer hall has long been a place to keep vigil.

Wooden shutters cover the small rectangular windows. Peeling blue paint exposes rough gray splintered wood. The morada's abandoned feel preserves the quiet dignity of the place. Planted in the ground, near an adobe wall, an imposing weathered cross stands sentry, black against the moonlit sky.

I settle on the steps of the old morada, leaning back to rest against a sturdy oak door. Clouds drift over jagged mountain peaks, slipping across the face of the moon. Stalking time for Coyote.

The steady low chant of long-ago prayer songs hangs on the night air from a time when men gathered during Easter week to walk in procession along dark country roads to this prayer hall, where they would mourn Christ's execution, grieve for his Mother Mary, and offer penance for mankind's sins. Here in this sanctuary Penitente Brothers practiced age-old rituals of purification.

And for me, this night, the old morada weaves its mystery. I drop into a place in my body, a place where time stops and the old ones come to call. My breathing deepens. I follow in the footsteps of the ancestors. Coyote yips. Owl hoots. The land breathes an answering call. Moon casts her silver light.

I find the courage to allow my nightmare images to resurface.

Several men wearing camouflage, holding machine guns raised to shoot, burst through the door of my second-grade classroom. The children and I hide behind bookshelves. We lie face down on the floor. The boy next to me has a tiny Scottish Terrier standing on his shoulder. I motion to the children to be very quiet. We are being hunted. The dream changes. The children and I are running hard across a field, running toward the river, searching for a place to hide. I am terribly frightened, desperate to keep the children safe. We reach a grove of huge cottonwood trees and crouch down curling into the dark ground. Here in the shadows, we are invisible. I place my finger to my lips, signaling to the children. Stay very quiet.

My dream offers a warning, a message of things to follow, betrayals. I know this to be true.

A soft glow lights the peaks of the snow-covered Sangre de Cristo Range as I stand to leave. I offer a prayer to family, to sanctuary, to all enduring spirits, for gifts of courage, stillness and protection.

Solvitur ambulando. *It is solved by walking.*

Magic Afoot

Early, not quite awake. Too early, I mumble as I stumble to the kitchen. Cats point to their empty dishes. Dogs, tails wagging, bound about grinning, eager to be outside. I trudge to the solarium and unlock the sliding-glass door. I step outside, my eyes pop open, my jaw drops. Dozens of colorful hot-air balloons float directly over the field below my house. Fog billows off the mountain, rises over ground. The atmosphere is surreal. I remember this is the weekend of the annual Taos Hot Air Balloon Fest. I had no idea they would coast over my house. I stand in the silky morning air. Brightly colored balloons fill the sky, flying so low some almost touch the rooftops. Whimsical whirring balloons. I wave to tiny humans floating in baskets overhead; they wave back.

Then I hear a familiar call. My heart skips a beat of joy. A flock of sandhill cranes break out of the mist, flying low. They slip gracefully between beautiful balloons in perfect V formation, on their annual fall migration to the Bosque del Apache National Wildlife Refuge in southern New Mexico. Without a thought, I stretch on tiptoe. My arms lift to join them. I am a child again, standing beside my mother, drawn outdoors by the cranes' haunting call echoing across time, from the tall-grass prairies and marshes of North Dakota to my home in New Mexico.

I run inside to phone my neighbor. Her recorder announces she will return my call. I know she is asleep. She calls later, "What did I miss?"

This afternoon I walk to a peace rally. Our mayor's words ring true. "Until we have peace in our hearts, we cannot know world peace, community peace, domestic peace. Until we have peace in our hearts, peace will elude us."

When I arrive home, my doggy friends lobby for a walk. Insist, actually. My mind is tied in knots. The rally was beautiful and well intentioned, but the day has changed. The mysterious quality of the morning — the astounding courage and beauty, the gut-level honesty of that larger world — is way gone. I am obsessed with the politics of the day. Who of us can say we walk with peace in our hearts?

Personally I entertain vindictive, manipulative, mean-spirited, violent thoughts daily. I chastise myself. I judge others. I am self-critical. And I get stuck there.

Dogs grin and wag and wiggle until I grab a jacket and my car keys. At the trailhead, I start a slow step up the side of the mountain. My thoughts weigh me down.

Max and Hopi Girl frolic ahead, totally present to their world. I am gone. My mind wrapped around my projections. I have no understanding of why, but I won't let go. I hold on fiercely to my nasty thoughts. Somehow this makes me feel important.

Suddenly, I wake up. Just above me on a cliff edge beside a gnarled old juniper, under a stunning blue sky, a plain rock cross stands. Three rocks in balance. I climb closer to find more figures. Each holds magic.

I try my hand. I build rock figures on ledges and in crevices. Some, I place on tree limbs. This play of balance involves all my attention — a joyful pursuit. Each figure evokes its own presence, a presence alive with energy and grace. Peace figures I call them.

Later I walk the trail to the peaks. I enter my dogs' world. We race, darting around bush and rock, playing tag. Their lovely, intelligent faces are alive with delight. We play for hours; I merge with the land so completely my mind expands, dissolves into this larger world, finding my way back to the language of true grace.

I saw them first many Novembers ago and heard their triumphant trumpet calls, a hundred or more sandhill cranes riding south on a thermal above the Río Grande Valley, and that day, their effortless flight and their brassy music got into my soul.

CHARLES KURALT

Bosque del Apache
National Wildlife Refuge

My dreaming mind whispers, *snow.* I crack an eye. Silver light filters through lace curtains. I burrow deeper under the comforter. My face crashes into my youngest cat, Catman, purring on a pillow. He reaches with his paw to pat my nose. Yorkie snuggles on my other side. Max and Hopi Girl stretch up from their fleece pads on the floor and lean their chins on the edge of my bed, waiting, waiting.

I swing my feet out from under the warm covers and pull on my robe. Our little parade marches to the front porch. Tree branches bend over the path to my house like old white skeletons coming to call. Snow falls. So beautifully quiet.

Come on down! Come on down would be my usual response. Today, though, I am driving to the Bosque del Apache National Wildlife Refuge in Southern New Mexico. Clear the roads. Clear the roads. I mutter.

Bosque del Apache, Woods of the Apache — named for long-ago Apache tribes who routinely camped in cottonwood groves along the shores of Río Grande/Río Bravo.

Bosque del Apache NWR is known as one of the most spectacular refuges in North America. Tens of thousands of migrating birds — including sandhill cranes, Arctic geese, and raptors, as well as year-round resident creatures — call this refuge their winter home.

Before jetty jacks, levees and upstream dams channeled the river system, the Río Grande meandered across a mile-wide flood plain. Stands of cottonwoods and willows — separated by sandy beaches, mud flats, meadows and marshes — created a mosaic, a diversely rich riparian environment.

Human impact — constricting, channeling, damming, straightening the río's natural meander — has resulted in a faster flow, eroding banks and causing a siltier river. Valuable habitat is lost — wetlands and marshes from Colorado to New Mexico to Texas and beyond, to the Gulf of Mexico — important rest stops for migratory and resident species, no longer naturally occur. Or they have been drained to support development. The magnificent bosque bordering the river no longer reseeds. The cottonwoods are artifacts. The once powerful Río Grande is now one of the most endangered rivers in North America.

The Bosque del Apache NWR, located on the northern edge of the Chihuahuan Desert, straddles the Río Grande. Habitat restoration is ongoing: thousands of acres of reclaimed shallow wetlands model the old river's floodplain, providing food, shelter and rest for migratory birds, resident birds and other animals. Staff and local farmers plant alfalfa and corn on the refuge, harvesting the alfalfa and leaving the corn for wild-life. Staff and volunteers plant winter wheat, clover and native plants as additional foods.

Thousands of sandhill cranes, snow geese, raptors, shore-birds and songbirds arrive in late fall, winging their way across the skies, following rivers and wetlands on their annual migra-tion to points south.

Walking the refuge soothes my soul, brings me back to reality, to the more-than-human world. The refuge rings with ancient rituals. One morning, I watch waves of silver light in an otherwise blue sky. Serpentine patterns weave like a silken banner then return to traditional V formation.

I ask at the visitor center what they might be. Pelicans, they tell me. Pelicans? I also learn that in a migration pattern, no one calls out orders. When one leader tires, another member takes over. All leaders. True community.

Two crows perch on the railroad tracks bordering the refuge. They appear to be deep in conversation as I drive by on my way to the wetlands. I catch a glimpse of several sand-hill cranes across the tracks. I park on the side of the road and crawl into a ditch. I crouch behind a patch of dry brush. I wait on my side of the tracks. Sentinel cranes strike up a stress call, an alarm to members of their flock feeding in the nearby wetland. The raised alarm causes several cranes to fly, using valuable energy reserves. I scurry off to my car chastised by my disrespect. I am guilty of what I so dislike in our human species, acting as though all creatures, land and water, are there for my entertainment, my use, my gawking, my photographs.

During the winter, fifteen to eighteen thousand sandhill cranes are among the fifty thousand animals migrating to the Bosque del Apache to join the resident population of birds, mammals and insects.

A little coot races across the surface of a marsh; an eagle perches on a snag. Cranes dance on the shores of far-off marshes. A red-tailed hawk sails overhead; a tiny mouse scoots for cover. A stalking coyote. A sleeping muskrat. The music of wildness plays in the air. I walk along the river, walking in the slow rhythm of time.

Just before sunup, I stand on the shores of a shallow pond. Freezing cold! I have been told this is the place to be, and the time to be here. Other humans are here, too — every one quiet. Flocks of sandhill cranes and snow geese have been roosting in the water all night, dreaming their winter dreams. With the first glow of light on the horizon, a flurry of wings, a roar. Thousands of snow geese lift off. Sandhill cranes move more slowly, lifting off in groups, rather than all at once. Dark wings sweep overhead. An energy stirs deep in my belly; my heart takes a leap. Spontaneously I stretch, reach my arms to the sky, and take flight.

And so they live and have their being — these cranes —
not in the constricted present,
but in the wider reaches of evolutionary time.

ALDO LEOPOLD
Sand County Almanac

Homeground

It has been said we come from the stars. My body and yours — all bodies — contain three grams of bright silver-white magnesium and smaller amounts of manganese and copper. Imagine.

There are elements of star within us all.

New Year's Eve. I settle in at my favorite B&B in Magdalena. A small herd of horses gathers in the pasture behind the bunkhouse. I walk outdoors to join them. Shades of magenta splash across the endless skies. Blue mist hangs over far-off horizons. Scarlet hues deepen to violet, to indigo. A perfect line of brilliant pink spreads along the edge where earth and sky meet. I stand with the horses as the setting sun drops behind the hills.

Stars pierce dark skies. I feel very small standing here in this great space. My mind leaps to grasp the knowledge that we Earth creatures carry the same elements found in stars. Certain cultures believe their ancestors *came* from the stars: Sky beings become Earth beings for a time, then return to the sky; life is circular, connected, expansive. Standing here wrapped in stars, I am convinced that this way of knowing stands open if we choose to be there.

I recall a story from my childhood, a folktale told by my grandmother, of a star who fell to Earth to become a water lily. I paid special attention to water lilies after that. When my brother and I sat on our porch roof at night, I wondered if water lilies returned to the sky as stars. I imagined water lilies, ivory petals shape-shifting to sparkling star arms, sailing out of the marsh, into the sky to join zillions of other stars. In those evenings while my brother and I waited on the porch roof for his elf friend, Elmer, I wanted to run to the marsh. Would I find the pond empty of water lilies?

Lee and Lori invite me to join them for New Year's dinner: crab legs, champagne and candlelight. A family tradition. The soft curves of the Magdalena mountains cradle the ranch, golden prairie flows into the dark blue of a far-off mountain range, to the edge of the horizon where stars fall to ground.

Way of the Labyrinth

We follow a wide shallow stream along a white-sand beach. Dragonflies skim low over sparkling water, iridescent green bodies reflecting light. Steep pink stone walls radiate age. Lush ferns, willow and cottonwood whisper an old language. I stop to listen.

Our three dogs grin with delight exploring secrets held in the shadows beneath the trees. Side canyons meander off the main inviting us to explore hidden corridors. We venture into a sheer walled maze to enter a time rift. Intriguing twists and turns lead us further into a labyrinth of red rock. The silence is intense. We have walked away from traveled paths into Earth's mystery.

A warning crack of thunder causes me to look up. Swirling dark clouds drop into the canyon. A flash of lightning follows. The storm moves in, suddenly upon us. Sleet and rain blow through the canyon, fast and cold. Although we carry rain gear, we are drenched before we zip open our packs. The once-sunlit canyon is now terrifying, dark and dangerous.

We are pelted by sharp sheets of rain as we struggle to climb over slippery boulders seeking shelter, thinking flash flood. *Can that happen here?* I wonder. A sense of urgency propels us. We race for high ground. Two of our dogs, although spooked by lightning and thunder, are young and move easily with us. My older dog is stretched to the limit. We lift her over boulders, push her along, sometimes carrying her. We are lost, disoriented by the rain, by the changing light, by the maze of canyons we had skipped into so casually.

Lightning reflects off the high walls of the darkened canyon. Thunder booms. The ground shudders. Exhausted and soaked, we duck under a shallow rock ledge. Edging along the wall, I find an opening. We crawl into a small dry cave. We curl gratefully against the rough curved walls to rest and wait out the storm. We open our packs pulling out warm clothes, food and water. Our dogs gather close, leaning into us and each other, for comfort.

We are quiet, grateful to be here. Lightning dances over the canyon floor. Sheets of rain pound the ground just feet away. I am shaken by the absolute power of nature, reminded once again of the fragility of the superficial grid we impose over reality.

A spider hangs out near the ceiling of the cave, at home in her web. We have entered her world. I know very little about spiders, never paid much attention to their differences, or names, but I do know that this tiny creature has lived Earth's life for 300 million years or so. Now with time to observe the complicated design of her web, I am filled with admiration. Her sturdy habitat is a work of art.

Grandmother Spider. Mythology reveres her as the powerful creative force bringing worlds to birth with thought.

Thought Woman/Spider Woman spins the web of life. As a strand within the web, each creature holds a place on Earth. Native people acknowledge her teachings through story, prayer, ritual and ceremony. Spider signifies healing of the soul, recovery from fragmentation. Her harmonious home is a living testimony to function and beauty, shelter and food. The wonderful detail of her web defines interconnection.

Navajo weavings reflect her teaching. Traditional designs reflect patterns of Earth: Endurance. Strength. Beauty. Spider's gift to her people.

Time spent in beauty. The dogs nap. My friend writes in his journal. After an hour or so, the storm calms.

We wend our way through a labyrinth of rain-streaked rock to the main canyon. Patches of mist rise from smooth slickrock. Burnished afternoon light sets the canyon rim afire. The air, pungent with the scent of sage and earth, feels soft against my skin.

The music of a flute echoes off canyon walls.

We walk through a cathedral of light.

Will You Walk With Me?

"Will you walk with me?"

With her silken thread Grandmother Spider builds bridges, calls us home. Her spiral or labyrinth design has long been revered as a symbol of pilgrimage, the path returning to the source.

A labyrinth's concentric structure reflects the energy of the universe. Fêng shui teaches that electromagnetic forces circulate beneath Earth's crust as wavelike currents, ensuring the balance of Heaven and Earth. Ancient Pueblo people etched spiral and web on sandstone walls. A circle manifests healing, a return to harmony. Traditional Navajo build their hogans round, attuned to the sphere of Earth. The sacred circle — Tibetan mandalas, an underground kiva, the chakra system, council circles, caves, swallow's nests, flowers, Sun, Moon, Earth, the planetary system, our own inner center, hara, belly wisdom.

In *Crossing to Avalon,* Jean Shinoda Bolen writes:

In the coolness and dimmed light of the thick-walled cathedral, one can imagine being in an enormous high-ceilinged ritual cave, with its stalagmite and stalactite columns, and mysterious labyrinth in the floor. This symbol of earth, and the Goddess, can be found not just here at Chartres, but in at least twenty cathedrals throughout Europe.

The Chartres labyrinth is geometrically designed to generate energy. Approximately forty-two feet in diameter, the labyrinth at Chartres was laid into the cathedral floor sometime between 1194 and 1220. The six-petaled rose in the center symbolizes the feminine.

At the time of Jean Bolen's pilgrimage, folding chairs completely covered the labyrinth. In order to walk the labyrinth Jean Bolen writes, "I removed the chairs one by one."

A ceremony in itself.

Several years ago, two friends and I embarked on a pilgrimage to San Francisco, to walk Grace Cathedral's labyrinth. We drove through the night. We parked the car in the underground parking lot of our hotel and left it there. We walked miles through the heart of downtown San Francisco to reach the Cathedral. Parts of this journey were challenging indeed. We walked a gauntlet of emotion, commercialism, smoldering anger. Despair hung out in the shadows leaning against urine-stained brick. Loss followed us, slinking along as a reminder. Beauty, too, in the hills and the sea.

Morning and evening, we walked with it all — the beauty, the hostility, the insanity, and the despair. We walked the labyrinth of the streets of San Francisco.

Grace Cathedral covers one square city block. Two labyrinths, one indoors, also hidden under folding chairs, the other outdoors, both modeled after the labyrinth in Chartres.

The outdoor labyrinth is part of a courtyard. Comfortable benches placed along curved adobe walls invite contemplation. We chose to be outdoors. We walked our ceremonial walk, or we watched others. We meditated in the center with fellow pilgrims. We walked with despair, hostility, and anger. We walked with serenity, and play, and great beauty.

On one circuit, I entered the center with a very tiny child who immediately flopped down on her belly, and grinned up at me. She patted the ground indicating I do the same. I did. Immediately my perspective changed. Here was the wisdom I sought. In this place, on my belly, touching ground with this small Sage, I was totally present.

"For us life is shrouded in mystery and the world defies explanation ... humans do not need to know everything there is to be known. The human past we feel is a universal past. No one can claim it and no one can ever know it completely."

RINA SWENTZELL
Santa Clara Pueblo

A Spiral Etched on Stone

The spirit of an ancient Pueblo culture can still be felt throughout the Southwest. Their architectural sophistication testifies to a people well attuned to the complexities of their environment. Atop mesas; under cliff overhangs; in large, inaccessible caves; or rising naturally from desert ground, thousands of Pueblo sites housing spirits blend graciously with the land.

For most of today I walk in rain, an arduous hike of more than eight miles. Flocks of sheep and herds of fierce-looking longhorn cattle graze along the steep cliffsides.

This evening is clear. As twilight settles, I pitch my tent in an oasis of cottonwood and willow. A raven swoops low, the whisk of his wings brushes softly in the light air. Blue lizards with yellow feet scamper on nearby rocks. Far off, lightning pierces the darkening sky.

Protected by a remote location, sheltered by overhanging cliffs, this particular Pueblo village is one of the best preserved in the Southwest.

Earlier today, I walked through sun-warmed rooms, imagining the everyday activities of a long-ago people's lives.

Tonight I prowl for hours, energized by the blessed solitude, the glittering sky. Finally, I pull my sleeping bag out of my tent and drop onto the ground to dream.

I dream I am walking across a wide sand canyon toward a stone village. The village appears as a mirage. I am carrying my shoes. My bare feet sink deep into the hot white sand; I walk toward a slab of stone in the cliff face: a spiral, carefully placed, near a crescent moon. Inward to center — a journey.

I follow in the steps of an older self, a story whispered on the wind, etched in stone.

I follow to begin again.

In Wilderness Lives
the Spirit of Integrity, the Essence
We Seek to Recover

Howl Your Morning Wild

I wake this morning to a profound silence. A soft, diffused light fills my bedroom. I see from my window the Sangre de Cristo Range shrouded in mist and clouds. Dark peaks seem to drift in the swirling, heavy gray mist, eerily lit by a rising sun.

I jump out of bed, throw on a jacket. Startled by my somewhat manic activity, four dogs follow me downstairs and out the door. I raise my face to the misty morning. Snow falls sweet and cold on my tongue. The ground around my house and toward the mountain is dusted in white. Blue spruce, ponderosa pine and scrub oak are frosted with ice. Below my house, the wide valley boasts another world: dazzling green sage-covered fields, blue skies, billowy white clouds, a tender golden light.

We take our walk, my dogs and I, toward the shadowed mountain. We howl our ecstasy. We run. We sniff and scratch. We mark our territory high and low. We are very rowdy.

Our neighbors, the coyotes denning on the banks of the creek—who normally lord it over my dogs by proclaiming their superior hunting skills with wild yips, yowls and leaping hoots—are silent.

Usually this early, we are more subdued. Candles glow. Coffee brews. I breakfast at a table placed in front of a long window facing the mountains and let the day slowly seep into my bones. The dogs patrol their boundaries, check for intruders, return to enjoy a quiet breakfast and nap.

This morning the mountain calls.

We are back at the house before 9 a.m. Bright sun glistens off snowcapped peaks, spilling over onto snow-covered grounds, burning off the mist, revealing tender shoots of green.

Crystals shimmer everywhere: in the trees, on rocky slopes, on sage and grass, in our eyes.

Land of Blue-Sky People

U te Indian bands who first settled here called this valley the Land of the Blue-Sky People, a sun-drenched landscape encircled in a mandala of mountains, forests, hoodoo rocks, and streams. Exquisite land, inhabited by a few folks and abundant wildlife. The Río Grande National Forest makes up two thirds of Saguache County, the county within the valley I call home.

Baca Grande, where I live, is in the foothills of the eastern slope of the Sangre de Cristo Range of the Rocky Mountains. These foothills extend to the floor of the San Luis Valley, five thousand square miles of sage-covered rolling hills, abundant aquifers, and canyons. Streams, birthed in the high tundra of venerable peaks, run deep and clear.

The towering granite peaks of the Sangre de Cristo Range provide refuge for my pilgrimage. This afternoon, I follow an old jeep trail toward Cottonwood Creek trailhead.

Some weeks ago along this trail, I turned to see a cougar nonchalantly walking a quarter mile or so behind me. Not wishing to experience an encounter, I whistled to my dogs, who bounded ahead happily unaware. Quietly, quickly we slipped on down through the trees toward home.

Today, starting up Cottonwood trail, I watch an eagle sailing thermals overhead. She sweeps in great arcs, drifts out of sight toward the higher peaks, returns to soar near puffy layers of cloud. I stop to eat lunch in a small meadow carpeted with wildflowers. Insects hum and sing, going about their life's work. Songbirds flit from flower to tree, feeding from a banquet of insects. Chances are, a bear munches berries in the brush, unseen by me. She likes it this way, for a bear is a private animal.

My body breathes deeply, grateful to be here. Quiet is exquisite. Solitude a blessing. I rest on a ledge overlooking a valley misted in blue haze. Time no longer exists.

I lie on the warm ground, eyes closed, absorbing the silence, the sun, my wild joy. In the distance, the Great Sand Dunes' shimmering sand hills float over the Earth. Shades of gold rise and dance on waves of heat. Above, the golden eagle soars.

There is a mountain walk, and a mountain flow,
and there is a time when the mountain
gives birth to a mountain child.

JOAN HALIFAX
The Fruitful Darkness

Mindfulness

Mindfulness comes with the climb.

My dogs and I walk along a gravel road toward the mountain, shadowy figures moving through heavy snow. Swirling clouds open to reveal the mountain's fierce face. I stop in my tracks, cautioned by her power.

Mist closes around us. We continue upward, turning onto a mountain trail where the silent forest waits, clothed in white. We follow the sound of a lively creek, where silver fir, graceful aspen and cottonwood drink. We walk through a forest of twisted old trees, home to guardian spirits. Gradually I disappear into the energy of the place, the eerie light, the order of the mountain. I disappear to listen to the sound of Earth dreaming. Dancing waterfalls, clear pools, tangles of fallen logs, rushing rapids, sheer moss-covered rock walls whisper their dreams.

What I discover is this: When you disappear, when you stop to listen, you will find your sorrow. It is there in your face, strangely beautiful. You are frightened by the sorrow, the sorrow where the river would be.

* * *

Crooked red-moss roots frolic beneath the surface of a fast-moving creek. A hobbit's grotto — rich with the scent of humid earth, bright with scarlet and gold leaves — beckons. We enter, silly as a pack of pups. Ancient boulders, covered in lichen, seem as carefully placed as a small Stonehenge. High above, a slant of sun glances through dense mist, touches an alpine meadow thick with birch and aspen setting off a golden flame. Craggy faces peer from rocks and thick old tree trunks. I look upward to bare mountain tundra, where rivers are birthed.

Last night I dreamed a river. In the dream I drive my dark-blue jeep up a treacherous narrow road above tree line to barren and cold tundra. Finally I can go no further. Huge boulders block my way. I climb out of the jeep to walk a winding trail leading further up the mountain. A Rocky Mountain sheep trail, I think. I notice a pool of steaming water under a ridge of rock near the peak of the mountain. A trickle of water as slim and bright as quicksilver dances past the pool. I can feel how young this small stream of water is, how fresh, and yet I know she is as old as time. I slide onto my belly to drink. The water tastes of life. I undress and slip into the steaming pool.

Far View

I follow a trail along a stream. Beneath the icy surface, water flows fast and clear. Round black stones, burnished smooth by rushing water, emit an ebony glow. The trail climbs steadily upward. My far view expands. I imagine soaring over a prehistoric sea where graceful blue whales leap and play, smile, and call my name. Dolphin laughs. Wily red dragons romp with mythical sea monsters thrashing ocean depths into a frenzy of whirling storms. Energy ripples through my body. I soar in a mandala of wild sea and indigo skies.

Delicate snow crystals, bright golden leaves, dandelion puffs, cottonwood seeds, sea and winged creatures dance their intricate song.

A great gray owl swoops out of the woods. Instantly the atmosphere is electric. Owl glides toward a branch near the top of an old cottonwood. A breeze ruffles her feathers. Her fierce amber eyes stare me down.

* * *

Shrouded in mists, bits of gold, and streaks of rain, the mountain flaunts a double rainbow. Coyote slips from the shelter of
prairie grass. Three pups follow at her heels. They head toward
the creek on the other side of the road. I stop my vehicle so
they can cross uninterrupted. They watch me, sharp eyes alert.
The sunset over the La Garita range glints off their sandy fur,
point hairs gilded in gold. We study one another. They, at
home on their ground. I, encased in my vehicle. Laughter rings
in the air. Then all four scamper off.

Flickers of gold flash through the sage.

* * *

My dogs and I tramp through knee-high snow. On a rocky
ridge just above the creek, a coyote skull gleams white. Austere.
I crawl through scrub oak and red willow for a closer look.
Coyote's spine lies further back on bare ground. I search for leg
and pelvis. I search for the intricacy of her life.

Later, while I sit with her bones, Coyote's holy dream
finds my heart and calls me home to roam desert, forest, sagebrush hills. As Coyote, I slip through a jack-pine forest unno-
ticed, camouflaged by my earth-colored coat. I make no sound
as I hurry over frozen ground, carrying Rabbit. I am tired from
a night of hunting. When I reach the shelter of my den, I nestle
down in grassy warmth, cradling my pups, offering food. We
gather close to fall asleep, to dream. Dreaming earth wild.

* * *

I carry your bones near my heart, wild kin. Phantom pups
scamper along the path as I hurry along the trail. A snowstorm
builds rapidly to the north, cuts fast across the valley tailed by
strong north winds. A streak of violet light hangs over the San

Juan range. For just a moment, each snowflake glitters like dragon's gold — then, a blast of wind whips the world into a frenzy. Chased by hail-like pellets I run toward home. My dogs race through the woods, eager for shelter. We stomp on the porch, shaking off snow. I gather wood to build a fire. A hearty stew bubbles in the Crock-Pot. I place Coyote's perfect bones on a bit of fleece.

Outside, a blizzard rages; snow covers the ground.

Down by the creek, Coyote calls.

Trickster

Coyote watches. Coyote, the wise girl, taps me on the shoulder to challenge my most precious beliefs. She laughs at me, her handsome face curious.

Coyote endures. She slips through the woods, toward her creekside den where she hides her young, a catch in her mouth. She watches from behind a cactus in the desert moonlight. She romps in mountain meadows among wildflowers, teaching her young to hunt, to laugh. She leaves her tracks in the sand, in our souls, waiting for us to catch up to life.

* * *

Some Native folks tell a story about a wandering anthropologist who came across a coyote in a trap.

"Please let me out of the trap. If you do, I'll give you lots of money," Coyote said.

"Well, I'm not sure. Will you tell me a story too?" asked the professor.

"Sure I will," Coyote shrugged. "I'll tell you a true story, a real long one for your books."

The anthropologist sprang the trap, collected a big handful of bills from Coyote, then set up his tape machine. Coyote rubbed her sore legs. She told a long story that lasted until the tape ran out. Then she ran off. The anthropologist went home and told his wife what had happened. She wouldn't believe him. When he reached into his pocket to show her the money, all that came out was a handful of dirt. When he played his tape for the other professors, the only thing in the machine was a pile of coyote droppings.

Coyote strips us of proud knowledge.

Strips us bare.

Coyote. God's dog.

The Way of the Mountain

Formidable thunder clouds roll over the Sangre de Cristo peaks, darkening the rocky slopes beneath the mountain's jagged spine. Flashes of lightning cut through black storm clouds. Mist drifts over the ground. I throw open windows and doors to be close to the storm. The electrified atmosphere carries the deep tones of Tibetan bells. Below my house, in the valley, sunlight glints off piñon and juniper. Then, in a moment, all is dark, the air goes dense. Fierce winds, thunder, sheets of rain and hail chase my dogs under beds and into closets. The full force of the storm hits. I race around, closing windows and doors.

The storm drifts across the valley. A rainbow arcs over the Sangre de Cristo Range. My dogs and I leave our house to walk a narrow rocky road cut into the side of the mountain. We climb toward a favorite place, a Buddhist shrine on the lip of a limestone bluff overlooking the valley. Fields of wildflowers draw dragonflies blue as the New Mexico sky. Nighthawks swoop, sounding off, celebrating. Mr. Pika chatters from a nearby boulder. Far off, over the San Juan Mountains, thunder rumbles. Flashes of lightning crackle. From his perch on the banks of Cottonwood Creek, Coyote calls, setting off a chorus.

An eagle circles. Sighting prey, he dives. Three mule deer munch rain-washed grasses in the woods bordering the road.

Our valley is known by some as a place of "mysterious sightings." Mystery does live here in the form of all wild creatures, in the faces of tiny flowers, in the wisdom of great old trees and rocks, in the transforming light, in the golden temple I walk toward tonight.

Mystery lives in the silver mist hanging over the valley, in the fire-breathing dragons at play in the sky above the San Juan Range. The dragons' antics capture my attention. One dragon, the one with the flirtatious grin, casts a burst of flame across the valley directly toward the great mountain, Sierra Blanca. Blanca catches the flame and roars her greeting. The ground shakes. Out of the swirling silver mists, Blanca appears, in a halo of firelight, her strong white face luminous.

The birds have vanished into the sky,
and now the last cloud drains away.
We sit together, the mountain and me,
until only the mountain remains.

LI PO (701-762)

In the Presence of the Mountain

Snow lies over the land. The rocky ledge where I rest catches the morning sun. A red-tailed hawk soars. The icy peaks of the San Juan Mountain range float in blue light. I doze, drifting into dreamtime. In the enormous velvet midnight of the eternal void, ancestral mothers dream, gathering to dream earth wild, to dream oceans clear. In the flaming heart of Earth, exuberant women spin dreams to life. And in their dreams, songbirds sing their forests wild. Star people dance across midnight skies. Old Mother Moon gazes over mountain ridges.

A long line of women walk the labyrinth, opening their hearts to life. Shattered hearts come together at the core, cradled by the grandmothers, wise women, together dreaming. In the flaming heart at the center, stories burn. Dreams are born.

* * *

On a high rocky ridge, Cougar suns herself, holding her babies dear. Cougar dreams her land wild, dreams steep cliffs and deep cool caves. Wolf walks unseen through forests of pine, cedar, tall white aspen, juniper. Wolf dreams his ground remote, his rivers clear; dreams his pack vigorous, his young healthy. Sky creatures nest in tall trees or on jagged rock crevices dreaming air pure.

On the mountain, Spider weaves her age-old dreams of worlds becoming, dissolving. For this is her way. If you are here to listen, Spider teaches respect. This is her work. She is unsentimental. You either find the truth or you don't. Pay attention, Spider warns, for Spider loves the mountain.

The mountain rings with Coyote's dreams, she who sings high praise and travels proudly with her young. Listen carefully. This is what you have been waiting for. This is why your broken heart cries. Listen to her song.

If you pay attention during the heat of the day to the scent of sun buried in Earth, your senses come alive with memory. You remember Earth holds your dreams.

Be still. Listen.

Inside the mountain, deep in her heart, Bear dreams her young to birth. Bear dreams creeks where fat trout swim, and the shores of creeks where blueberry bushes ripen. Bear dreams ground rich with grubs. She dreams sweet-smelling tall-grass meadows, wildflowers, spring rain.

Muskrat and Beaver, two fine old seers, relate their dreams for wetlands to a circle of young. A cool breeze, carrying the scent of ground cover and snow, drifts through the crowded circle. Fur thickens and grows heavy. Food is gathered. Dens are built, strong and sturdy. You remember, don't you? Once you were there, listening to your dreams.

The mountain holds dreams, dreams of wild ones who come to drink in cold rushing streams, who later dream on beds of dark-green moss. The mountain dreams for wild ones who dream for one another. Dreaming their Earth wild.

On the mountain, weathered boulders rumble ancient dreams of a time when all creatures danced as radiant beams of light, knowing their place on this Earth. And will again.

If you go to the mountain take only a little of yourself.

Revealing the Sensuous Body

The woods near my home offer endless opportunity for exploration. Today I walk a limestone ridge near a winding stream. This part of the stream is sheltered by tangles of willow, cottonwood, reeds and cattails. Fallen trees, burnished silver by weather and age, have been transformed into dragons, serpents, goblins. I am cautioned by their tough old faces. Emerald pools nestle in shaded bogs hidden by jagged stone ridges. Cardinals nest here. Ravens croak their raspy love songs. Ruby-eyed spiders weave lacy webs, lay out glistening drops of amber nectar on rich green ferns to entice the thirsty white moth.

Snow-covered banks frame clear rushing streams. Small round copper stones shimmer in stream beds. I bask on a sun-drenched boulder. The stream's song echoes through my body. Light dances off the surface of the water, a wild fragile light. I feel sorrow rustle inside me like a trapped animal. My eyes blur from the sunlight. I close my eyes to dream.

Boundaries disappear.

I find myself padding silently along a trail. My tracks mark the trail. I bend over the stream to drink. A cougar's broad cat face mirrored in the silvery water returns my gaze, keen amber eyes focused, alert. How beautiful. I test my long legs, my lean, muscled body. I leap onto a cliff ridge hanging over the stream. My thick tawny coat glistens in the sun. I shake my fur. I snarl a little and stretch my body along the sun-warmed rock. I wrap my tail around my back legs. Purring, I sink into the warmth of the rock.

Invisible. At home.

The Land Remembers

Snow falls at around 9,000 feet, just above my home. Sheets of rain veil the valley below. My dogs peer out near dusk, sleet-gray mist covers the land, but the rain has stopped. Off we go, down the muddy road, toward the valley. We slosh through puddles, slipping, running, delighted to be out of the house.

Dense clouds part above the La Garita mountain range. Shades of scarlet shimmy across the valley to touch Mount Blanca. Her peaks sparkle. Flames of rosy light radiate from her steep rocky slopes. She burns from within, her rolling snow-swept foothills lustrous. I stop on the road, mesmerized by Blanca's beauty. The gray fog lifts, waves of liquid color — turquoise, blue, gold, magenta — sweep the skies.

We walk across a meadow tipped with spears of ice. My dogs bound ahead, rustling through silvery grass heading toward the river. Murmurs of old ones linger on the prairie. My bones hum with their rhythm. The ground vibrates with the rumble of thundering hooves.

The beat of thousands of hooves rings in the still air. And in the deep circles where buffalo wallowed, rolled, and kicked up their heels, ghost buffalo wallow still. From a cliff above the stream, Spirit Wolf calls her pack home. Shadow Wolf shakes her lovely silver-white coat, throws a piercing glance, turns on her heel and melts into a thick stand of aspen. The land remembers.

Keen eyes alert, Great Gray Owl watches. Hidden in a deep crevice of a tall cottonwood, she guards her nest, her chicks. She remembers tall grass prairies. She remembers buffalo, wolf, cougar. She remembers her fellow travelers.

High on a golden bluff above the river, Cougar rests, nursing her two cubs. She is thin from lack of food. Her prey starve, too. Drought. Competition for land. Guns.

The land remembers. Ghost Walker.

On this ground, where Blue Sky People once walked, their ghosts walk still.

If You Go to the Mountain
Take Only a Little of Yourself

A vital change of consciousness.

Integrity

Marking home. Marking territory. As you and I are familiar
with our neighborhoods — family, friends, a favorite coffee
shop, a market, a park for games or relaxation — other creatures,
too, cull out a territory, add comfort to a cranny, a warm patch
of ground, a crevice, a pond, a stand of trees. A den of pine
boughs, a nest of soft down, a beaver's lodge — all convey care,
the definition of home. Most creatures instinctually create a
safe place, often close to familiar territory where they were born.

Displacement, destruction of habitat, fright and confusion exhaust a creature, allowing no time for grace. An intact
ecosystem imprints upon a species. Mating rituals, migration
routes, known food sources, predator/prey relationships, hibernation, grooming rituals are written in a specie's DNA. For
many creatures, protecting their young rises from the deepest
instincts of their nature. When things are right there is time for
play, joy, exuberance.

Today I walk a river's meandering path. My two dogs, Charley and Little Bud, bound ahead. Bud catches a scent. Nose to the air he turns in to the meadow. Charley races to join him. Curious, I follow. In the center of the meadow, hidden by autumn's tall wheat-colored grasses, a young coyote has fallen, permanently stilled by a bullet. She rests on her side, cradled in a nest of grass, her fur ruffling in the light breeze. I kneel to caress her body, lovely even in death, fur thick and glossy, all colors of autumn, brown and gold and black.

Is this the playful girl, the beautiful girl I have watched throughout the summer? She who leaped in joy, so awesomely at home, marking territory, perfecting her hunting skills. Why would someone shoot her? No houses are near, no fence containing precious ownership rights. Just one easy shot stopped her dance forever. Just one act of cowardly malice. Violation. We mourn, my dogs and I, sitting by her in the grasses. Charley and Little Bud recognize violation. They recognize betrayal of territory. I wonder at abuse. How casually we kill. I wonder at how thoughtlessly we violate another creature's territory, how carelessly we fragment the integrity of habitat, of body and soul. Where is the fury?

We, the human species, are due a vital change in consciousness. We have lost our grounding. Fragmented, insecure, we assault those who are vulnerable to our thoughtless arrogance. Poisons, guns, noisy machines kill the light in ponds, rivers, forests, animals, in our eyes. Where is the fury? Where is our passionate voice? Intimidated, we speak in modulated tone, so dulled by what is deemed appropriate behavior. Where is the fury?

Unbecoming, is it? Fury in the face of betrayal is frightening to those who seek approval. Terrorist acts go on. Coyote is killed by whatever whim serves those who worship gun or trap or poison. Wolves are killed in New Mexico, Wyoming, Idaho, Minnesota. Bodies buried; whispered deaths earn bragging rights. In Alaska, wolves chased by planes fall from exhaustion, easy prey, shot where they fall, from the air. Wolves are killed for fur, for fun, or just because the name Wolf justifies the killing. Wolf, a keystone species, absolutely essential to ecological integrity, recently removed from the endangered-species list, can now be shot on sight.

Bear, Mink, Beaver, Cougar — nothing is exempt. A yearling bear cub may be hunted in many states. Does this require any skill? A cub, curious as a child rambling through the forest. An adult bear hibernating — shot in his den. Killing beauty takes no courage, only a small ego, a gun, and a fat hunter with an ATV. A bull elk, a majestic creature, shot for his antlers, body left to rot. Trophies are displayed. Prairie dogs poisoned, a creature essential to an ecosystem — tunneling, aerating soil, releasing moisture into the atmosphere, calling down the rain.

Is it because our fellow creatures are so integral, so at home in their environment, so embodied with spirit? Are they so threatening in their supple grace, their finely tuned genetic intelligence, to a species who has broken its covenant with Earth? What are we modeling for our children? This love of killing. Violation cuts deep into our psyches, our hearts, our nerves. Ignored, violation grows large…a rigid, fragmenting, controlling, seductive, greedy shadow feeds upon our healthy nature, our playful spirit. And when acts of violation touch the heart cold we lose all feeling.

Violation comes in many forms. Violation of territory challenges us on a daily basis, from societal worship of the weapon to corporations trashing our oceans, our forests, our land; chemicals, plastics, fertilizers, pesticides, oil spills—leaching into water, soil, air.

We dig into Earth's heart, narrowing habitat necessary for territory, quiet, nourishment, rest. We give little thought to the fragility of our planet or to fellow inhabitants on this planet. Oxygen, the very essence of life, is manifested by tiny plankton in the oceans. Yet islands of floating waste, commercial fishing and chemicals destroy plankton as well as the ocean's delicate balance. Ocean creatures, creatures of an intelligence beyond our understanding, die in polluted waters, lose their way due to sonar testing, are caught in illegal fishing nets.

Most of us are blissfully unaware, in denial, or supportive of territorial violence; therefore we are guilty in this chemical war against our planet. Chemicals suck the life from our cells, our psyches, our souls until instinctive wisdom dies. What we do to air, water and land ends up in our bodies. We become the chemical, the weapon, the violation.

We walk with ghosts. Ghosts of true integrity. Ghosts of such beauty and grace our hearts are bereft with the loss. Ghosts of silver-tipped Wolf, Grizzly, Prairie Dog, Jaguar, Panther, Buffalo; ghosts of rivers running wild. Native cultures call from beyond walls we have erected to protect the shallowness of our way of life. In our hubris, we have given ourselves permission.

We abuse our own species, our most vulnerable. Our way of life is breaking down, and we ignore despair. We have torn our ground apart. We wonder why we feel so fragmented. We have lost our connection to our core, our integrity. Our children drug themselves with chemicals, pornography and guns. They kill. They walk into the bottle. We wring our hands and ask why.

We glimpse the lengthening shadows of ghostly travelers as they walk away to the sanctuary of the heart, or climb the ladders to the stars. They take with them instinctual intelligence, perceptions and power, knowledge and experience acquired through generations. They carry away their stories, their wisdom, their rituals. They carry away continuity, community, the integrity of walking their ground. The integrity of knowing their place on this Earth.

Bruce Chatwin writes in *The Songlines:* "The man who went Walkabout was making a ritual journey. He trod in the footsteps of his Ancestor. He sang the Ancestor's stanzas without changing a word or note, and so recreated Creation." The labyrinths or invisible pathways, the tracks of the ancestors across the continent of Australia, were by lineage territorial boundaries. A person's song was his way of keeping his world, and the larger world, alive.

The Aboriginal walked the Earth knowing his place.

The songlines are now bulldozed.

A person's song was his way of keeping the world alive. Instead, we have fallen in love with, as Ed Abbey writes in *Science With a Human Face,* "the plastic-aluminum electronic-computerized technology forming around us, constricting our lives to the dimensions of the machine, divorcing our bodies and souls from the earth, harassing us constantly with its petty and haywire demands."

The Aboriginals' bulldozed songlines live on in the shadows of our hearts, reminding us of lost rituals across the planet — connection to migratory corridors, pathways to water, birthing and nesting grounds, cultural rituals…

Facing violation requires waking up. Requires stepping out of the conciliatory mind so approved by society. Taking action. Naming violation requires courage, a warrior spirit. The good little girl? Or boy? Let them go — they have always been a hindrance.

We are at the edge of truth, a truth that calls for a drastic shift in consciousness.

Your voice be heard.

For Bear

The Birthing Dream

One night I dream I discover a cave hidden behind a waterfall. The cave entrance is partially covered by a morning glory vine. Inside the cave, a golden brown bear sleeps on a bed of moss and pine needles. She has shoved trees trunks into the dirt ceiling. Bear's heartbeat fills the cave. I see she is pregnant. I curl down on the bed of moss close to her.

Bear, with her great heart and wise old soul, is Mother. In the timeless world of mythology, caves represent the womb of creation. This is literally so for Bear. In her sturdy den, she births and nurses her tiny cubs.

So for those of us beyond the boundaries of civilization dreaming for Earth, dream for Bear, dream Earth wild. Dream Bear's territories remote and far-reaching. Imagine revealing your own untamed heart, revealing your great heart to Earth and Bear and to those who are her companions on the edge of time.

Once upon a time and long ago, storytellers told how Bear pierces the thin veil between worlds with her tongue, opening the way for us to follow, crossing borders into the larger world where wildness dreams.

*My connection to the natural world is my
connection to self—erotic, mysterious and whole.*

Terry Tempest Williams

A Rhythm in My Blood

A Rhythm in my Blood, Old as Time.

When we take time for solitude and nourishment, when we follow our deepest instincts, the world says: "How strange, how odd. My, My."

The world shakes its head and races on by, a blur of frenzy and importance.

In our cave we laugh emitting soft growls of contentment.

We lick our paws and groom our fur, slowly rubbing our large furry self against cool cave walls.

We snooze for a while. We chew and gnaw for a bit. We roll on our backs to gaze at the rough cave ceiling.

We build a nest of grasses and flowers on the soft gray dirt of our cave floor.

Later, much later — maybe weeks or months later — we emerge. We step out onto our cave ledge to sniff the air, to bask gratefully on sunbaked earth. We shake vigorously to fluff our fur, our point hairs golden in sun-spun air. We smell of soil, cavelike, scrumptious, delectable. We are hungry.

We test our roar.

We are powerfully alive.

We are Bear. We are Woman.

Woman and Bear, the wildness within.

We have forgotten we are Bear. We have forgotten we are Woman. So eager to please. Watch how you quiet your voice. Watch your mind go dizzy, shut down. Watch how your body performs. Watch layers of denial fall over your truth… as a deadly fog. You wonder who you are. You struggle to find your place.

Our truth lives at the edge of memory, deep in the womb. Our truth lives here at the core, in this place of power, of creation, of mystery.

Bring your breath here. Breathe this place in your body, this healing place. Can you feel the energy? Your walk starts here on sunbaked Earth. With Bear.

If you choose to be here, in this place of integrity, you can never go back.

Mark of the Bear

Walk unseen, Grizzly Bear.
Walk untouched, Grizzly Bear. Solitary kin.
Silver-tipped giant.
Run fast and free, Great Bear. The integrity of wild lands
flows in your blood.
Teach your young to hold wild, to hold fierce their territory.
Claim your place, Grandmother Bear.
And in your long winter dreams, dream Earth wild.
For your young. For our young.

Our hearts have grown too small for Bear. In the lower
forty-eight states, small islands of grizzly exist. Black bears fight
for survival as all wilderness shrinks. Meadows, canyons, mountains are bladed, clear cut, erased to build gray subdivisions
and their attendants — Walmart, Pizza Hut, McDonald's, Taco
Bell — insuring the death of nature, our primal nature.

Weakened bear populations, a barometer for all life, reflect disastrous habitat invasion. Monumental human arrogance invades wildlife boundaries, closing corridors of movement, fragmenting territory until each fragment is isolated, unhealthy, static.

Bear requires wild country, seclusion. A resourceful hunter, she stays fat and healthy feeding on salmon, grubs, vegetables, berries, plants. Her sharp claws are well adapted to dig deep for ants and rodents. Good nutrition prepares her for breeding, for hibernation, for bearing healthy cubs.

A mother bear trains her young through play and sound discipline. Healthy animals at play build strong muscles, practice hunting skills, social skills. Bear teaches her young to follow her instruction. Bear requires a healthy ecosystem, time, privacy. To teach her young, a mother bear requires territory to roam and feed and rest. In a healthy family system, members enjoy endless hours of interaction. Stressed animals flee from habitat invasion, logging, snowmobiles, roads, guns. An animal on the run suffers confusion, distress, exhaustion.

Humans, too, require a healthy ecosystem. Look for the sorrow in our children's eyes. Look for the confusion. It is there. A spontaneous interactive environment encourages play, training for life skills. Serenity. Calm. Instead, television blares one act of violence after another. Our children turn on to pornography, dished up as entertainment. Addicted to a beat not their own, our children stare blankly at video games, bodies tense, mechanical, manipulating games of war, violence, sex.

Imagine young at play, active, alive, interested — involved hearts afire with joy. Newborn calves romp. Colts kick up their heels and prance in lush meadows. Puppies grin, eyes alight with mischief. Bear cubs tumble along a trail following Mom. Wolf and coyote pups chase sticks, play tag, wrestle. All are trained to pay attention. Survival depends on remaining alert to Mom's voice. Animals begin early to practice life skills, to explore social behavior. Clear communication is essential; wariness, an art. Posture, voice and body contact offer immediate feedback to feelings and mood. In the animal world, every gesture is meaningful.

Some years ago in Yellowstone National Park, I watched a grizzly cub claim his territory under a canopy of old cottonwoods near the river. He seemed very young, inexperienced, somewhat puzzled. For a while, he sat on his haunches and leaned his back against a tree. He seemed to be contemplating this turn of events. Perhaps Mom had been injured or killed. Perhaps she had signaled the end of his childrearing.

Whatever happened, he was on his own.

Young as he was, he understood his need for protection. He claimed territory near the river across from a well-traveled tourist road. Male grizzlies will attack the young. Rarely, though, would an adult grizzly venture this close to civilization.

On the road where I stood, more than a hundred people jostled, cameras poised, to view a wild animal. However, without a blink, most would shoot a bear who ventured too close to their home; or shop at a Walmart, built on land that consumed wildlife habitat. How odd, I thought, the juxtaposition of eagerness/ignorance at work here. A world so out of balance.

A wild meadow, home to elk, bear, cougar, wild turkey, pheasant — home to countless critters — a place so heartbreakingly beautiful that each time I walked there I lost myself in the integrity of a more-than-human world. Walmart wanted this meadow. We protested for years. "A Super Walmart sits fifteen minutes down the road," we pointed out.

Eventually, though, inevitably, the Walmart was built, "tastefully" sporting a mountain theme. Paved roads and cement parking lots strangled the land. Like weeds, fast-food joints and gas stations sprouted. Homes were built, too, on a hill above the shopping place. The meadow is gone.

Is it ever in our hearts to remember we are one strand in the tapestry?

I watched the little bear for a long time in his attempt to declare his territory. I watched as he scraped his paw, claws long and sharp, down the bark of a lone pine. The mark of the bear. He's got moxie, I sighed. I prayed that his share of moxie was substantial, Mom's teaching strong.

What this young grizzly knows instinctually has been called down from his ancestors. He knows survival as a wild creature, the challenges he faces in the wilderness. What he cannot comprehend, what cannot be carried from his ancestors, is the dangers he will face from humans and our continuous exploitation of Earth, our complete lack of respect for territory. He does not know Pine Ridge Development Inc. Quail Run Golf Resort. Bubba's Construction Co. Cheney Oil. Wilderness Exploitation. He does not know that we arrogant humans (the two-year-old on the planet) want it all. He does not know the poacher who will shoot a denning bear, a sleeping bear. He does not know our brokenness.

*How much would you give to know the truth you
hold in your broken heart?*

At the Edge of Truth There Is Hesitancy

A longing stirs and you drop to the deeper lost regions of yourself, to a memory so ancient your broken heart cries. Wait here.

Here is the language you remember.

The place where genius lives.

A young wolf hoots as in a dream. He seems to be planted right here, under your bedroom window. You draw a breath to that sacred place where grief lies heavy. You call out to him. With a flick of tail he is gone.

If we still lived with wolf, the door would stand open to the mind of creation. If we still revered Grandmother Spider, we would know that all life is interwoven. If we still lived among bears, we would know our wild ancestor as a mentor for spiritual renewal.

Medicine bear. Earth's wild god, the great grizzly, is gone. If we still lived among bears and wolves, elk and spotted owl, if we still lived among wild creatures, we would know to listen to our heart's cry. If we still lived with free-flowing rivers and wild forests, we would know the mysterious alchemy of life.

How do we find our way? we ask.

Look to where you are, an older self suggests.

Begin with the heart.

The place where genius lives.

The wind, the rain, the mountains and rivers,
the woodlands and meadows and all their wild inhabitants;
we need these perhaps more for our soul than
for our physical survival.

THOMAS BERRY
The Dream of the Earth

In the Time of Rivers and Wolves

What dreams may come if we entered the dream of the Earth? What dreams may come if we opened to humility?

What dreams may come if we allowed ourselves to grow deep, revealing the wind-tossed, sunbaked, rain-washed enduring spirit found in wild open spaces?

At night beneath the moon, a river dreams, introducing the flower, the bird, the sky, the fish, the insects, the animals, the trees, the moment.

At night beneath the moon, a river dreams the promise of community.

The oldest dreams of Earth are water. A single droplet holds life. Fluid. Clear. Reflective.

Intricate.

A film of water envelops Earth, as a newborn.

Protective.

"What dreams may come" if we "set in to the work of truth?"*

What dreams may come if our thoughts were with the river and the wolf. What dreams may come if we envisioned a life of heart and grace and motion? What dreams may come if we explored the experience of the present moment?

What dreams may come if integrity guided our decisions?

At night beneath the moon, a young wolf dreams the broken pieces of his land whole.

At night beneath the moon, a young wolf dreams the promise of continuity.

What dreams may come if we honored our sacred compact with Earth and merged our dreams with Wolf and River, as keepers of Earth, as keepers of the laws of nature?

What dreams may come in the time of rivers and wolves?

What dreams may come if we regarded Earth's sensuous body as our sacred body?

Something true.

What dreams may come if we lived from this place?

What might the river, the wolf, think of us then?

---

*"What dreams may come?" (Shakespeare, from *Hamlet*); "set in to the work of truth" (Heidegger).

The Bone and Soul Spirit of Wilderness

Some say that going to the wilderness is coming home. Once again I walk the windswept shore of this immense lake, a sea of a lake, linking the borders of northern Minnesota and Canada.

November is cold. Icy winter. We walk the deserted shore, my dogs and I. Low gray clouds carry snow. The air, heavy with moisture, carries the musky scent of water and light.

Water and light, the tarnished color of old silver. I listen for voices that might invite me to enter a world where wildness dreams. I listen for a song I carry in my blood. I set aside the distancing murmurings in my head that would separate me from this place. I follow a memory from childhood of a time I walked the shores of the Lake of the Woods with my grandmother. A memory of a wolf just at dawn, silver coat caught by light, calling to his mates across a strip of water from where we stood. "How wonderful," my grandmother whispered.

On the shore where I walk, mammoth chunks of drift-wood polished clean and smooth by wind and water rise out of the rough sand dunes, some with the look of dragon or turtle, fish or dinosaur. They tower over the landscape, otherworldly sentinels, burnished silver. I come upon them cautiously. I am not prepared for their fierce presence, the power of age.

I walk this rib of land, this sandy strip of beach, mind deepening to the texture and rhythm of Earth's sensuous nature.

Wolf tracks stand out in stark relief pressed deep into the moist sand. A perfect line of wolf tracks, larger than my hand, intermingle with beaver and fox, elk and deer and moose.

Welcome home, I call to my dogs. Welcome home to a blessed place where humans are outnumbered by dark untamed waters, dense forests and wild creatures.

Welcome home to the bone and soul spirit of wilderness. Welcome home, I shout. I stand at the edge of the dark woods on the shores of this immense lake. I envision wolves, fluid as breath, moving through the forest. Invisible.

I follow in the tracks of wolf. I walk the shore of this great lake invisible as wolf.

My body transparent as the mist. Wolf blood courses through my veins.

I practice this state of being invisible, intimate with the land, something true moving me, no need to be seen.

Who are we really anyway? Muscled water, fueled by light.

The dogs are all about play — racing waves, chasing, splashing, bumping each other straight into the joy of total surrender. They are dizzy with delight. They dance with waves, they shake drops of water into the air. Water catches light…

When I look out over the lake I see…beauty undimin-
ished, power untamed, a formidable, raw landscape. I know
about the depth, the stormy waters, the fierceness, the steep
cliff faces where there is no shore, only solid unyielding stone.
I know about the guardians who watch over the lake, about the
graceful wild ones who keep this place as home. I know about
the golden eagles who nest nearby. I know about the great lives
who swim beneath the surface.

The lake calls me home to stand with mystery once
more…to peel off civilization. To breathe again in the space
between water and light.

Moving, changing…
like the elements themselves…open renewed.
Winding inward to the core.
Time for intimacy to grow.
Creation lives here, in the space between water and light.
Mystery.
An energy field, the balance so fine, so delicate.
Can you feel it —
the spirit of play?

In the Space Between Water and Light

Mystery. The light in a wolf's eyes. The dancing energy of a wild river.

Mystery. The river at night in winter. Under the snow the ice sounds.

Mystery. The patience of the land eroding slowly, with time to renew again.

Mystery. When the wind stops. Listen. Can you hear the river shimmering in the space between water and light?

Mystery. The air that connects a flock of birds during migration acts like a muscle, unites the individuals into a group — the group soul. When one leader tires, another takes her place.

All leaders. True community.

Mystery. A mountain full of age and water and crystals and roots. Breathing deep and slow, encircling a valley of water and light. A mandala.

Mystery. A river flows, all grace, curving, dancing, wearing away, moving around, leaping over obstacles…breathing, breathing…

Mystery. Starlight over a dark lake going on forever.

Mystery. You are, fundamentally, muscled water fueled by light, reflections of light.

Luminous…all grace.

The spirit at play.

Mystery.

Isle Royale

Bitter cold winds whirl out of the north. We coast through the rough waters of Lake Superior to our destination, Isle Royale. Huge waves spray the deck of the passenger boat we boarded in Grand Portage. Layered from head to toe in wool and down, a yellow rain poncho and an orange life jacket, I am chilled to the bone. At last we put in to land. We are surrounded by what seems to me an ocean.

Lake Superior is the largest body of fresh water in the world, more than thirty thousand square miles of deep, stormy waters. Thirteen hundred feet deep in places. Not a placid lake at all. This is North Country, the lake and the island make up part of the Canadian Shield. Wild country.

My companions and I are involved in a natural-history seminar. Our primary focus: wolf. We will spend two weeks in camp on Isle Royale, a northland wilderness microcosm.

In the early 1900s, Isle Royale had been devastated by massive logging. When logging operations were set up and the primal forests — white spruce, white pine, balsam fir — cut down, loss of habitat wiped out woodland caribou as well as other species native to the island. Over the years, second-growth vegetation colonized the island — birch, poplar, shrubs, small balsams, undergrowth; moose, coyotes, beavers, rabbits, birds, rodents, waterfowl, deer, grouse found this tangled sanctuary to their liking.

In 1940, Isle Royale was designated a national park. No more hunting or logging. To stabilize moose populations a farsighted group of naturalists and wildlife biologists advocated for the introduction of wolves.

Wolf — keystone species — essential to sustaining a healthy ecosystem. Necessary to restore Isle Royale's ecological balance.

Without waiting for the politics of humans, lone wolves and breeding pairs crossed over from Canada, reintroducing themselves. As wolves established territory, their numbers increased, packs formed. Isle Royale and its inhabitants entered a complex ever-changing balance of predator and prey.

All predatory animals have an important role in the natural world, taking down the weak, old or injured, thus insuring the strongest, most genetically sound will breed. Man has reversed this process by taking down the trophy prize — often only retrieving antlers or head as bragging rights, or the hide, the fur, to feed the fashion industry. Small egos striving to be noticed.

At the time of our study, over two hundred square miles of land forested with aspen, birch, fir, spruce, and lodgepole pine, as well as ground cover, provided ideal territory for wolf and fellow inhabitants. Territory for denning and birthing. Territory for hunting, shelter, rest, and play.

For me this was a personal pilgrimage, a quest to walk in the tracks of a fellow creature whose intelligence, grace and endurance I admired. We set up camp. Our equipment was mediocre at best, definitely not the super slick, lightweight, or ultra functional we find today. This was the late seventies, after all. Camping meant roughing it.

* * *

Vacationers are about, as well as ferociously hungry black flies and the famous moose-sized island mosquito. Still, I spend hours at the beaver ponds. A small head swims into view. A beaver paddles toward his lodge and emerges from the water, dripping. He walks onto the bank in a sort of upright crawl, a wad of mud tucked under his chin, the mud held secure with his front paws. He plops the mud into place on the lodge roof, turns back toward the pond and swims off. Before long another beaver, a lodge mate, appears with a log in tow, crawls onto land pulling the log and adds it to the tangle that forms the roof of the lodge. As he slides back into the pond he slaps the water with his tail.

One day, two beavers team up to pull a log out of the water onto land and carry it to its place with the others.

The young saplings whose bark the beavers eat are also added to the tangled woodpile of the lodge.

The beavers are curious about me, too. They swim by with a glance and a slap of tail toward the bank where I sit swaddled in a long-sleeved shirt, droopy hat and long pants.

My days with the beavers endear them to me forever. They are a model of nature's integrity, their ponds home to uncountable species. I mourn the dynamited lodges I encounter now in the Southwest where wetlands and meadows once flourished, enriching soil and plant life, creating habitat for waterfowl and other wildlife, cycling moisture into the atmosphere.

My campmates and I have lived through two days of pelting rain. All but one of our flimsy pup tents have collapsed. Seven of us sleep huddled together in the one sagging tent that remains upright. Our sleeping bags take on the look of submerged hippopotami. We are unable to light our puny little stoves. We have no dry wood. No coffee! At one point in total desperation, I chew coffee grounds.

This is our sixth morning. I wake, ecstatic, to the promise of clear skies. I climb to a shelf of rock overlooking a wide bay. Canada geese, mallards, mergansers, coots, loons, shorebirds and waders sleep among the reeds and cattails. Across the bay, a thin band of pale-pink dawn light deepens to salmon, fires a blaze of scarlet over tall white cliffs jutting out from shimmering waters. Dark lines cross the face of huge cliffs marking ancient shores, marking a time when the depth of Lake Superior was even greater than it is today. A time when dire wolves, whooping cranes, great sea creatures and woolly mammoth ruled the day.

Beyond the cliffs, the forested hills throw off the night's mist.

A trail curves around the bay to the far white cliffs. I strip off layers of damp clothes as I climb to reach a ledge to lie naked on sun-warmed rock. Sky and water extend as far as I can see, impossibly blue. The far horizon seems to me to define the edge of this place, and the world beyond. Lazily I ponder edges. What would that be, to walk the line of my vision, along the edge of my imagination? How would life be lived?

I fall asleep to dream a great golden panther curled around a sleeping baby. Protective. This panther, my talisman, has reoccurred as a dream figure ever since I was a tiny girl.

Forested hills beyond the cliffs call to me. I throw on my dry clothes. My boots sink into a carpet of moss and pine needles. The air is humid, heavily scented with pine and musky moist earth. Woodpeckers busily hammer out their homes. Horseflies attack. Mosquitoes rise from the ground in hungry swarms. Blue jays bring down the sky. Wildflowers bloom.

I wander, somewhat lost, in the hollows of the hills. A patch of maverick strawberries catches my eye. I kneel on the moist ground to pluck strawberries warmed by sun. I cup them in my hands, cradling the rich earthy scent of home. I bite into the wild, and shiver with delight.

We listen to their songs each night but no one in our group has sighted a wolf. Signs of their presence, yes. Wolf prints on the shore, tracks on the trail, a coarse tuft of hair snagged by a pine branch. Healthy herds of deer and moose. A shadow in the forest.

One afternoon I stroll along a well-worn trail deep in thought. I pause, unable to comprehend what appears to be a tiny animal skeleton imprinted in the earth. A deer? I wonder. A perfect skeleton pressed into the soil. What happened here?

I place my hand on the ground where the bones rest.

All is quiet.

*If all the beasts were gone, men would die from a
great loneliness of spirit, for whatever happens to the
beasts also happens to the man. All things are connected.
Whatever befalls the earth befalls the sons of earth.*

CHIEF SEATTLE OF THE SUQUAMISH TRIBE
quoted from a letter to President Franklin Pierce

Yellowstone Wolves

Imagine a wolf pack readying for the hunt. The alpha
calls her pack together. Tail wagging and muzzle licking
reunite the pack into one powerful unit. A chorus of
piercing howls voice exhilaration. Single file, they glide
through the forest. Scenting animal prey, strong bodies move
into action. Trusting the guidance of their leader, the pack
spreads out, each takes a position to close in for the kill. An
old bull moose stands his ground. He too has confidence in
his strength.

Snow sticks to our boots, our jackets, eyelashes. Heavy fat
flakes fall straight down. Our tracks are covered in moments.

Two friends and I stand on a ridge overlooking the Yellowstone River, eyes pressed to our binoculars. We have driven from Colorado to Yellowstone National Park in northwestern Wyoming to visit the wolves. Across the river a pack of wolves walk single file toward a pine forest, dark fur coated white, nearly invisible in this snowy world. We are seeing the Lamar Valley Pack, one of several wolf packs inhabiting this wilderness.

Yellowstone National Park contains 2.2 million acres of wilderness; a rich biodiversity of lakes, mountains, pine forests, meadows and wetlands well suited for wolves as well as bison, cougar, coyote, bear, elk, deer, raptors, beaver, small mammals, fish, songbirds and insects. Here wildlife is protected from the human predator as long as they do not cross the boundaries of the national park.

Reintroduction in the mid-1990s of fifteen gray wolves imported from Canada realized, for the first time in seventy years, the return of the wolf to Yellowstone. The park offered a perfect laboratory for studying the impact of a keystone species. No one could have predicted that in the years since their arrival the wolves of Yellowstone would reshape an entire ecosystem.

Pups from the original fifteen matured to form new packs. Wolf packs in their natural habitat stalk elk and deer. Unaccustomed to a top predator, herds of Yellowstone elk and deer congregated near rivers and streams, calmly munching tender new shoots of cottonwood, willow and aspen. The hunting prowess of wolf packs soon penetrated their serenity, and they moved to higher, open ground. No longer a delicacy for elk and deer, riparian vegetation matured to full growth, shading streams and rivers, cooling waterways to temperatures favored by trout and other freshwater fish.

In 1996 beaver colonies were nonexistent. Thanks to riparian recovery, beavers returned, building dams and lodges. Beaver dams create marshland habitat for plants, otter, musk-rat, mink, duck, insects, reptiles, migratory and resident birds —an intricate ecosystem. For the first time in seventy years, Yellowstone appears to be evolving to a time when flora and fauna are kept in balance dictated by the forces of nature.

A wolf claims her territory, she seeks a mate. When their pups are grown, some will form their own packs. They will need territory. Where will they go? A wolf who crosses the boundaries of Yellowstone is more often than not a dead wolf. We want it all.

Human overpopulation is unchecked by any kind of common sense or understanding of Earth's delicate balance. Overpopulation is now a politically incorrect subject. Why?

Human beings fail to understand the basics of ecology. Each species maintains integrity within a specific ecosystem. The war on wolves is one symptom of an overall sickness called ignorance. The wolf is not the only target. The same folks who carry out the elimination of the wolf call down the same fate on bison, grizzly, cougar, and any other animal or culture standing in their destructive path. Endangered. Wolf struggles to reclaim territory, appearing where we do not expect, in our dreams.

Wolf crosses boundaries to open our hearts.

Wolf Tracks in My Heart

My cabin sits on a rocky ridge just above a strip of beach. Graceful willow, cattails, pine and white birch circle the shore, a vast sweep of unspoiled wilderness. Across the bay, thousands of acres of dense pine forest covers the land. I see no signs of civilization.

Early one morning I enjoy coffee on the open porch. Mist drifts over the still lake and through the trees. I particularly love this time of day. Before sunrise, before the mist burns off, silence is deep. Tempo, slow. Contemplation comes easy.

Suddenly I hear crashing sounds from across the bay, a powerful splash. Clouds of mist obscure my view, but something swims my way. A dark form splashes out of the water, touches ground panting heavily and leaps forward toward the shelter of the forest. An elk? A moose? I wonder.

In the next moment a wolf bounds onto shore. I catch a glimpse of her as she pauses to shake herself. She is gorgeous!

I can't believe my eyes. A wolf in the wild, perhaps thirty feet from my cabin.

She lopes off, her easy gait accelerating to a full run. I am aware of how charged my body feels, every cell alert to the sounds of the two animals racing through the forest. Sunrise burns through the haze.

The wolf returns, her silver coat flashes light; her prey may have swung around, stood his ground, sent her packing. She prances on the shore, races in the shallow water, sending rainbows into the air. In a flash, she is gone. I watch until I see her climb the white cliffs across the bay. She stands silhouetted in sky for a moment then melts into the shadows of her forest.

You must have been playing, you beautiful girl, I say softly. That night, in a dream, I stand at the edge of a forest. A pack of wolves walks single file across a meadow, toward the woods. They are strong and healthy; their fur all colors of white, gray, silver, black, brown. Each one passes where I stand; their amber eyes glow with intelligence. They disappear into the mists. I hesitate, then follow.

Entering a World Where Wildness Dreams

I dream I am standing at the edge of a circular clearing. White cliffs gleam in the moonlight. The cliff walls, weathered by wind and rain and time, are carved deep with caves. Flowering bushes shelter the caves. Wolf pups peer from each cave opening, lovely baby faces curious, alert. The circle seems to form a labyrinth, with one wolf at the center. I enter the labyrinth and walk toward her. She wraps a tapestry of woven wolf hair around my shoulders. The shawl covers me lightly.

Again, a dream of Wolf; beyond the boundaries of civilization, a feral invisibility. I know this place in my body. This place where wildness dreams.

* * *

Moonlight vanishes into a snowy sky. A tiny light shines from the window of the one cabin close by. All other signs of land, trees, shrubs or fences dissolve. The scent of pine blends in the mist with the slight odor of feral wolf.

Even in full daylight wolves have an ethereal transparency, a spirit-like quality. I have a longing to be in the presence of this quality. I have chosen to be here as a volunteer — to learn from the wolves how to live with integrity.

Mission: Wolf is a wolf sanctuary in Southern Colorado. Here, wolves live in packs in half-acre fenced enclosures; some are sent to live here by their human, who fell in love with a wolf pup but found that a grown wolf is not a pet. Many of the wolves have suffered manifold cruelty: rescues from fur farms, from chains, whips and cages. A human-imprinted wolf cannot be returned to the wild. This spells disaster for the wolf, whose natural instincts have been dulled by an unnatural environment.

And so they are here — to live their lives in captivity — stressed from stories we will never know. Yet, in their eyes lives the mystique of their wild ancestors. At the edge of dreamtime, ghost wolves walk, shoulder to shoulder, inviting, encouraging their wounded fellows.

The staff at *Mission: Wolf* is dedicated, caring, and knowledgeable. Education is a primary focus. I am encouraged to spend time with the wolves, watching from outside their enclosures, where shaded hills, piñon, grasses and shrubs create an environment for play, shelter, solitude, rendezvous. Wolves are social animals governed by the rules of the pack. The strength of the alpha determines the strength of the pack. As much as possible a compatible pack environment is modeled at *Mission: Wolf.*

Today I watch wolves wrestle, touch muzzles, relax or nap — each one alert to my presence. At one point, the alpha leaps up, rests his enormous paws on the fence, and gives me a piercing gaze, letting me know he is in charge. Wolves, as do most animals, communicate directly and clearly through body language: touch, smell, ears alert or flattened, eyes playful or fierce, voice — a whimper, snarl or howl — informing the intruder to pay attention, suggesting ways to approach...or not.

Some wolves arrive at the sanctuary too psychically wounded to live with mates or to have human visitors. Rowdy is one whose enclosure I stand before on one of my circuits of the sanctuary, a handsome white wolf who lives alone, a difficult state for a social animal.

Rowdy had lived in a small yard in the city. He jumped the fence one day and killed a neighbor's dog.

On the day I entered one pack's enclosure with a staff member, I was prepared to be greeted. And also to remember that this is wild-animal territory: stay attentive. This pack of wolves had certainly, by then, scouted me out in their keenly perceptive way, stripped away my pretense. They were curious for a closeup meet and greet. A wolf greeting ceremony is effusive. An important ritual. The alpha places huge front paws on my shoulders, sticks his tongue in my mouth, all the while grinning. Each wolf takes a turn. A wolf is extremely strong; however, they rub themselves against me lightly, touching in, fluid as a spring rain. They play-fight, they scent mark, they nip and chase one another, eyes full of playful mischief. Fully attuned to their ancestral heritage, my dogs do this, too, when greeting a human or animal friend. The visitor is expected to be complimented by this display of acceptance, and most are.

Wild creatures remind us: we are bound in a shared destiny. Is this why our species is so eager to take them down? We cannot bear to look at our folly. We want to think our wild fellows are separate from us...

There is no out there — no separateness.

In the Shadow of My Heart

I walk the rise of the horizon, the edge of a vast snow-covered land extending outward into the far beyond of the universe itself, with all its shadows and unknowns. Red-tinged canyons appear without warning, then fall away into darkness. I watch my step. Nothing here to ease my mind. The empty landscape pulls me open. There is a bit of terror in the silence, the great wide landscape. Even coyote snugs up quiet, curled for the night in his sun-warmed rock shelter.

The last light of a midwinter sunset casts shadows across the prairie. I walk toward home over ground where buffalo once ruled. Now ghost buffalo roam the prairie, rustle through tall grasses. On this shadowed prairie I walk with thousands of buffalo. Great herds of buffalo rumble through my body. I breathe their power. As moon rises above the horizon, I catch a glimpse of white. I kneel to touch a weathered skull cradling a nest of wildflowers.

A story, light as a heartbeat, brushes against my fingertips:

> *Everything the Kiowa owned came from the buffalo.*
> *Their tepees were made of buffalo hides; so were their*
> *clothes and moccasins. They ate buffalo meat.*
>
> *Their containers were made of hide, or of bladders*
> *or stomachs. The buffalo were the life of the Kiowa. Most*
> *of all, Buffalo was part of the Kiowa spiritual life.*
>
> *A white buffalo calf must be sacrificed at the sun*
> *dance. Priests used parts of the buffalo to make their*
> *prayers when they healed people or when they sang to the*
> *powers above. So, when the white men wanted to build*
> *railroads, or when they wanted to farm or raise cattle, the*
> *buffalo protected the Kiowa. They tore up the railroad*
> *tracks and the gardens. They chased the cattle off the*
> *ranges. The buffalo loved their people as much as the*
> *Kiowa loved them.*
>
> *The white men declared war on the buffalo, to wipe*
> *out the Kiowa's food source. They built forts in Kiowa*
> *country, and woolly headed buffalo soldiers (the Ninth*
> *and Tenth Cavalry was made up of black troops) shot the*
> *buffalo as fast as they could, but the buffalo kept coming*
> *on, even into the post cemetery at Fort Sill. Soldiers were*
> *not enough to hold them back. The white men hired*
> *hunters to do nothing but kill buffalo. The hunters ranged*
> *up and down the plains, shooting sometimes as many as a*
> *hundred buffalo a day. Behind them came the skinners*
> *with their wagons. They piled the hides and bones into the*
> *wagons until they were full, then took their loads to the*

new railway stations being built, shipping the buffalo products east, to market.

Sometimes the pile of bones stood as high as a man, stretching a mile along the railroad track. The buffalo saw their day was over. They could protect their people no longer. Sadly, the last remnant of the great herd gathered in council to decide what they would do.

The Kiowa were camped on the north side of Mount Scott, those who were still free. One young woman got up early in the morning. The dawn mist rose from Medicine Creek as she looked across the water. Peering through the haze, she saw the last buffalo herd appear like a spirit dream. Straight to Mount Scott, the leader of the herd walked. Behind him, came the cows and their calves, and the few young males who had survived. As the woman watched, the face of the mountain opened.

Inside Mount Scott, the world is green and fresh as it had been when she was a small girl. The rivers run clear, not red with blood. The wild plums are in blossom. Into this world of beauty the buffalo walked.*

Returning to the sanctuary of the heart.
At the edge of vision.

---

*Old Lady Horse, *Native American Testimony*, Penguin Books.

"*The wildness at the depths
of nature will shelter us.*"

A GYPSY FRIEND

Reverence

It is the evening of the full moon in July. I walk with a friend to a wild mountain lake nestled high in the back-country of the Sangre de Cristo Range. We climb a steep escarpment and dip downward following a gentle slope to the dark lake below.

On the rocky shores of this hidden lake, we listen to the great mountain sing her evening lullaby. We watch as she gives birth to the moon. Moonrise over the Sangre de Cristo Range. A timeless event. Her radiant silver glow backlights the mountain's spine long before her laughing face appears. We watch the curve of her tip over Crestone Peak. She moves fast over the jagged edge. The dark lake transforms, becomes liquid silver. My friend sparkles as if sprinkled with glitter. My heart shivers, knowing the miracle of being present on this Earth.

My friend and I walk to the crest of a nearby hill. We follow an elk trail. The bright full moon guides our pilgrimage. She whispers dreams of wild ones dancing in shadowed green forests, on red rock mesas, on shores of mountain lakes, on desert sands where the sky begins. She whispers dreams of invisible worlds where ancestors weave their dreams of prophecy, birthing worlds. She whispers dreams of power. Power alive in wild lands.

She whispers dreams of grace, the lithe grace of the great bear, of secretive panther, lynx and cougar. She whispers dreams of fox, badger, beaver and wolf. She whispers dreams of reverence.

The night carries the scent of Earth, Cedar, Pine and Juniper — like when rain first touches ground. And in our tracks, Cougar walks. She is unhurried. Curious. Her strong body carries dreams of mother moon. In her amber eyes, wild lands glow.

Song for an Elk*

On the morning of the first snow, a knife-edged profile of white dunes and one sun-illuminated cottonwood grove affirms our valley's ceaseless beauty. Autumn's color survives. Winter's snow softens.

Reverent silence is my best response. But the words *too much* come to my lips a few moments later when a herd of more than a hundred elk cross the road a few yards in front of me. I slow as I near another vehicle. Its solitary occupant, a hunter, gun rack across his truck's back window, has climbed from the cab of his truck with his camera. I wait as a teeming riot of legs and haunches surges over the fence into the field. My delight turns to horror. A half-grown elk calf remains trapped beneath the barbed-wire fence, one leg caught in an impossible tangle of three strong strands.

I jump out of the car. When I realize how strong the tight wires are, and see how terrified the thrashing animal is, I know I can't free it. I look toward the hunter who has returned to his truck. I flag him down. He grabs the only tool he has, a shovel. "Do you have a pliers?" he asks. I produce a weak facsimile from my car. When they fail to dent the tough wire, he attempts to dig up the fence post with his shovel.

Our presence and obvious distress frightens the elk calf even more, and a shrill cry of fear accompanies his thrashing. The angle of his leg arches unnaturally as he struggles to free it. The fence post is impervious to the hunter's effort. As luck would have it, this rancher maintains his fences better than anyone in the valley. The animal seems doomed to break its back or leg.

Unexpectedly, I begin to sing for the elk. Wordless sound escapes from my throat, a steady rhythm with no melody. The animal is immediately still. Startled, I let sound come from a place I do not know. Together the elk and I relax into the rhythm.

Another truck approaches. The ranch hands that maintain this fence jump out. Help is here. I quit singing. As more people approach, the animal again becomes agitated, thrashing and shrieking in alarm. I begin to sing again, and the elk is immediately calm.

The hunter takes the wire cutters the field hands provide and cuts the fence. One strand does nothing. Two strands and the elk stirs, sensing the possibility of liberation. As the third strand snaps, there is a tremendous whirling of legs and the lithe body, unharmed, bounds for freedom.

"That's about as close as I'll ever get," the hunter grins. No doubt, the saving of this life had been more thrilling than a kill.

"Did I hear you singing to that baby?" a woman asks.

"Yes," I admit, still stunned. Singing to the animal was not something I "knew" to do.

The song must have been the elk's, not mine.

*Written by Anne Silver and originally published in *Crestone Eagle*.

Serpent Fire

I dream I am hiking Colorado's backcountry. I climb a sage and piñon mesa. Hot sun bakes my skin brown. When I reach the plateau, I see a large black-and-white serpent coiled in the center. I step close and peer cautiously into the triangular-shaped face. I look over my shoulder. Another serpent follows along the path I had just walked. This serpent wears brilliant shades of green and gold. Beautiful. But I am concerned. I back away to the edge of the mesa. Both serpents follow.

* * *

A friend and I are on a road trip to Wind Cave National Park in South Dakota. We stop for coffee in a small Wyoming town and take a walk. In a field half mile or so out of town, an outcropping of white cliffs illuminated by morning's sun captures our attention. A fault in the midst of all this wide-open space. We crawl under a barbed fence, pushing through waist-high grass toward the jagged cliffs rising chalk white against the brilliant blue sky.

We climb the rocks. My friend spies a snake skin — shed, coiled, nestled in a patch of yellow daffodils, shaded by an old piñon. We kneel for a closer look. The shed is delicate, paper-thin and transparent, a gentle reminder. A reminder for our own journeys as we grow to shed and leave behind a skin grown too small. A reminder to become vulnerable over and over again.

We both ache to take the skin as trophy, but we leave it behind on natural ground.

Certain cultures honor the serpent as life-force energy, instinctual energy radiating in every atom in the universe. Kundalini, the feminine force, sleeps at the base of the spine.

Spiritual practitioners call up this power through their bodies in dance, through their voices in story, through meditation, drumming, prayer and breath. In ceremony.

My friend and I travel on to South Dakota. We camp in a small well-tended campground, fenced. In this National Park, the bison roam free. We spend our days walking through thick windswept grasses following the bison at a distance. As we wander over the land, pretense slips away; we fall into old time, bison time, when thousands of bison roamed tall-grass prairies. We let our bodies move as bison: heavy, powerful, grounded.

We watch bison immersed in billows of dust, rolling on their backs in wallows — bowl-shaped craters carved through years of bison wallowing — giving themselves a massage, rubbing off old clumps of fur.

How good it must feel, I think. How utterly and totally freeing. As soon as the buffalo move on, we walk across the plains to the wallows to do our buffalo imitation. Enjoy a dust massage. Shed old skin and fur.

It is here in Wind Cave National Park I see an eagle walking. I nudge my friend and whisper. "Do you see the little guy in the meadow over there?" We are on our daily meander, wending our way through stately grasses. We pause. I squint, unable to grasp what I am seeing. We scrunch down and wait. He walks closer. An eagle, I whisper. Is he hunting gopher, mice, perhaps young grouse? I didn't know they walked on the ground. For quite a long time we are still. At last, the eagle does a sort of run/hop and takes off.

Great wings fill the sky.

All around you in the bare trees
the dead and the unborn gather
waiting for what you will say.

MORGAN FARLEY
Poets Speak, Taos, New Mexico

Insomnia

As I often do when I am sleepless and vulnerable to fear, I walk outdoors. Cats and dogs follow. Stars glitter in dark skies. I throw a prayer to Earth's wild heart. I catch her tears.

We fight for what we love. We are in desperate need of wise guidance.

This morning, I read in the *Albuquerque Journal* about a recently released Mexican wolf, shot to death for killing a calf. Yesterday, I watched a tiny buff-colored calf romp on a golden hillside at sunset. Tonight, awake at 2 a.m., I am tortured by this dilemma. The complex issues around wildness and domesticity. The photo of the wolf's release leaps to mind. It captures forever her fluidity and grace. Her energy. Wild rivers flow in her body. Dense green forests. Tall-grass prairie. Ravens and hawks.

How would she know not to nab a calf? She was hunting for survival, by wits alone. She was not raised by a pack who would warn her. *Human! Danger!*

Was she on public land leased to the rancher? My land. Her land. I feel immense anger. A wolf needs hundreds of miles of territory. Without territory she is prey to the human.

Habitat destruction. I have just returned from a trip to Denver. Cherry Creek, once a free-flowing creek through what is now Denver, was for thousands of years a gathering place for elk and deer, wolf, beaver, and scores of prairie dwellers, including Native Americans. In the last forty years, the Cherry Creek shopping district has become a symbol of high fashion. A place to be seen. A place of wealth and indulgence. Silliness.

Without soul, Cherry Creek is little more than water diverted down a concrete channel, no longer a creek at all.

Imagine if you came home one night. Your house dynamited. Your grocery store bulldozed. Your bank bombed. Your children poisoned. All you knew was gone, with no way to start anew.

Where would you go?

I wonder if it's fair to the wolf, this program of reintroduction? Left to themselves they would make their way back from the brink of extinction. However, this would mean a radical change of consciousness in the human species. Barry Lopez writes. "It will require that we re-imagine our lives … it will require for many of us a humanity we have not yet mustered and a grace we were not aware we desired until we had tasted it."

Will we wake up in time to grow from the mentality of the two-year-old demanding his way? What will it take to bring us to a mature understanding of connection and community?

In spite of myself I laugh. The baby of the planet rules, the youngest, the one who throws the biggest tantrums. Our ignorance, our arrogance is astounding; our self-centered belief that everything belongs to us.

In *Sundog*, Jim Harrison's character Strang says it best: "The worst suffering I see back here in the States is another matter. People here suffer terribly without knowing why. They suffer because they live without energy."

We are desperate for wise guidance. Desperate to know our place.

Light slips over the mountain. Down to the river I go. I follow a winding path along the side of a cliff. On the muddy shore where red willows grow, I stop to watch a family of beavers rebuild their lodge.

In the beginning was the Word, and the Word was Change.

A.B. Guthrie Jr.

Springtime

This morning while I wait in the kitchen for the hiss of my little espresso maker, I stare out the window. Storm clouds roll down from the mountain, tumbling across the valley. It's 7 a.m. I feel as though I am standing in tar. Usually by this time, I am at work contemplating the blank page or jump-starting my writing day by fiddling with editing.

The dogs bustle at the solarium door, eager for breakfast. I step outside for a moment as they push past me to their food bowls. Sometimes when I am in this mood, I pace my yard, hoping for inspiration. This morning I pace, coffee cup in hand. Fog drifts over fields below my house. The first fat snowflakes touch ground. Mist shades the face of Taos Mountain. Suddenly the wind picks up. I shiver and hurry into my warm house.

Spring cleaning. The urge overtakes me. I sell furniture, clean closets, haul boxes of clothes and shoes to thrift stores.

I give away jewelry. February seems early for this, but I am compelled by a need for space, by a sense of being on the verge of something totally different.

We have just come through a difficult period. I have faced personal challenges. My young cat Sadie struggled on the brink of death.

Sadie came from an animal sanctuary in Utah.

In November a year ago, I visited the sanctuary and several weeks later returned as a volunteer. I noticed her the first day, hiding under a bench, her eyes the size of marbles. I asked about her and learned her story.

Sadie and her three newborn kittens were rescued from her makeshift shelter under a trailer near Kanab Creek. Their survival had depended on her fine hunting skills, her wariness. Somehow she managed to nurture her kittens despite fierce cold, threats from coyotes and other predators, including the human who reported to the sanctuary his intention to poison her.

Sadie's kittens were adopted immediately. She was placed in the feral cat unit of the sanctuary with little chance for adoption. The staff member I talked to warned me not to approach her. "Sometimes when they are so frightened they will attack," he said.

"What a courageous little cat," I thought. Each day I talked to her. I told her how much I admired her. One evening I brought her a fleece-lined basket. A place of her own. The following morning, as though it were the most natural thing in the world, I lifted her into my arms. What a sweetie pie! She snuggled, and purred and purred. That was it. I was hers.

However, the stress of homelessness, lack of a healthy diet, and nursing kittens had weakened her immune system.

This year, in December, a severe gum infection took hold, the pain so intense she could not eat. My veterinarian offered little hope for treatment and, therefore, her survival. "This can't be true," I said. "Sadie is not even two years old."

Fortunately for us, another veterinarian was more determined. She researched the internet for information. We embarked on a series of steroid injections; although the outcome remained uncertain we had reason for hope.

At home, I blended tuna and milk, coaxed Sadie to eat. She lapped small amounts of food but not enough for life. My heart was thin with worry.

One day she leaped onto my bed, unfazed by Yorkie's territorial claim. There she stayed for weeks, jumping down only to use her litter box. I placed her water dish and a plate of food on a towel on the bed each day. I bought cases of highly nutritious Nutri-Cal, the soothing consistency of honey, and fed her by hand.

My other animals recognized an emergency: Yorkie shared her precious space. Max and Hopi Girl peered over the edge of the bed, their sweet faces full of concern.

I researched feed stores, asked questions, told her story. People responded with their own animal stories, offered suggestions and encouragement.

She fought to live.

She was my teacher.

To lean, but more important, to be leaned on.
For that's what friendship's for.
To be loved, but to love.
Or what's the use?

To be generous toward life.
Else I lose myself.
Above all else, to care.

A.B. GUTHRIE, JR.
The Blue Hen's Chick: A Life in Context

Springtime. It is April. Magpies are building nests in the huge old cottonwoods below my house. They fly low across our yard, tilting down to warn the cats. Catman, nine months old, peers from under a lawn chair impressed by Sadie's feisty standoff with the birds.

Springtime. Literature from the Bosque del Apache National Wildlife Refuge poses the suggestion that cranes dance to release aggression. They do not need endless meetings and studies and surveys to know to do this. They follow age-old rituals of knowing as they dance with their mates for pure joy or to release aggression.

I play with the joy of dance. Instinctually my body remembers. I realize how we humans stiffen to hide our truth. I imagine a world of dancers fluid and supple. How strong we would be, how colorful and confident. I imagine possibilities. How fine it would be to redirect hate and fear and constant talk into dance. I imagine rebuilding communities, ecosystems, restoring life to our world. Now that's something worth dancing to celebrate!

Down to the river I go
to where the cranes dance.
Here is another world,
a larger mind.

The play of the river,
the soft blend of sound,
the cranes remind me
that life is so much more
than a human affair.

Springtime. The will to live. Sadie and I walked the edge together. Two lives. Two miracles.

Springtime. I drive to Ghost Ranch to walk the labyrinth. In the dusty center, someone has placed a moon shell. This is so unexpected, I grin, hold the shell to my ear, and listen to the sound of the sea. How remarkable — a shell carrying the sound of the sea to the desert. A pale rose shell, winding inward to the core.

When I return home I search my bookshelves for Anne Lindbergh's *Gift From the Sea.* She writes, "Solitude, says the moon shell. Center-down, say the Quaker saints." She quotes Rilke, "We are solitary. We may delude ourselves and act as though this were not so. But how much better it is to realize that we are, yes, even to begin by assuming it. Naturally we will turn giddy." Giddy!

I ponder solitude. I imagine the solitary seed of a cottonwood tree dropping onto the muddy shores of a wild river, taking root in dark soil. I imagine a tiny sapling lifting its face to the sky, supported by rich ground nutrients and sun and rain. Centering down. Becoming itself. I imagine a tree with sturdy branches and bright crackling leaves offering shelter to deer, a nesting place for birds, a limb for a spider's web, shade for a picnic. I imagine a lively cottonwood grove, where young and old flourish, where fallen leaves nourish the ground, a meadow where prairie grasses dip and sway, where shrubs, and willow grow thick, where small critters buzz and sing, where snakes burrow, where wetlands flourish. And a river flows wild and strong.

Springtime. My friend Amanda and I climb Copper Ridge. Amanda has a sketch in mind. I need to walk the land. At one point, after a torturous portion of the climb, we rest on a rocky ledge overlooking the Río Grande Valley. Light glints off tin roofs in quiet old villages nestled in high mountain valleys. The cut of the gorge meanders across the land as far as the eye can see. Amanda points to a shaded canyon in the rolling hills north of Ojo Caliente. "There is where we brought the sheep to graze, down from Vallecito. I rode behind my cousin on the back of his horse." She breathes a long sigh, remembering another way. We fall silent, nostalgic for a land that is all but gone. "People need wild places," I say softly. "That is what grounds us, keeps us humble."

I relay to Amanda a story told me by a friend who teaches second grade in Denver:

"One morning she placed a group of plastic animals on a table in her classroom. When the children arrived, they grabbed the small shapes, zoomed them in the air like rockets, crashed them into one another. Threw them at one another. Stomped on the little plastic pieces with angry violent jabs. Positioned them like guns and shot at one another.

"'They just want to kill,' my friend said to me in despair."

Amanda nods. We have both been classroom teachers.

"What will ground the children?" I ask Amanda.

We watch clouds of dust billow over acres of scraped ground east of Taos.

"Watch out for progress," I mutter. Amanda pulls her sketch pad and pencils from her pack.

I hike into the pines. A faded trail twists through the timber. To the west, the Sangre de Cristo Range cuts blue scallops across the sky. I pause to catch the voices of the land.

A red bird flies out of the trees. A marmot sings atop a small pile of dirt near the entrance to his branching burrow. Swallows touch up their cliffside nests. Potter wasps dive in and out of their clay-pot homes. Resident ants work their anthill — tunneling, hauling in food, repairing. A piñon jay and her mate carry sticks to reinforce their piney nest. Lizards bask on sun-warmed boulders. I cast my longings over the great distance to center deep in the hidden shadows of craggy peaks and blue valleys.

I dream a female black bear living in an alpine valley where clear streams flow strong and fast. I dream a female black bear awakening in her sturdy den, drawing her young close.

Springtime. A balmy evening in May. T-shirt weather. I attend a lecture at The Harwood Museum of Art with my friend Joe. A woman stands in the courtyard, waiting for her husband to park the car. She wears a floor-length coat of wolf fur. I look away.

Springtime. Camino de la Placita, one of the main streets for both tourist and local traffic, is cordoned off for construction. This will continue through spring and summer. Traffic is diverted to our narrow residential street. Nightmare bumper-to-bumper traffic disrupts the calm rhythm of our neighborhood. Rude, speeding, angry drivers careen by our homes, endangering animals, children, anyone in their path. Everything speeds up. My heart races, my brain feels ready to explode.

Springtime. The Bosque del Apache NWR. Before I leave for the Bosque, I walk down the hill behind my house to find Catman. He is in a trance, sniffing sage. I interrupt his musings when I pick him up to take him inside. Struck by a testosterone fit he fights to get loose, scratches me on the arm. This is my baby cat, who first carried the name Feather. Inside my house, neither of us very happy, he attempts a stare-down. He actually contemplates another attack.

My grandson Jake and I found Feather and his friend Skye. We were packing our gear into the car after a three-day float trip down the San Juan River when Jake noticed a small white kitten, perhaps two months old, playing in a field. I prayed the little guy belonged to someone. Anyone. No such luck. Oh well, I said to Jake, we'll take him back to Taos with us; someone will adopt him — a lovely white Siamese kitten with sky-blue eyes.

I paid our bill, walked out the door of the lodge and there, under a bush, sat the smallest kitten I have ever seen. Two children, their faces filled with concern, crouched nearby. They had given him a dish of milk, but they were traveling and couldn't take him. "Too hot. Mom said no." Jake appeared, and the four of us conferred. We'll bring him home with us, I assured the children. The little girl lifted the baby into her arms and handed him to me. He was light as a feather.

Jake and I outfitted the back seat of the car for the two kittens. Once they were settled I realized from their interaction that the older kitten had been caretaking the tiny one. He wrapped his arms around him and they slept all the way to Taos.

We played with names on the drive home. We agreed Skye was fitting for little blue eyes; but when I suggested

Feather for Feather, Jake was not sure. "What if its a boy?" he worried.

On the drive home, Feather and Skye became our kittens. Their joy filled my home. They played chase all through the house, raced across the tops of chairs, skidded on adobe floors. They practiced pouncing. One kitten would hide behind a door, under a chair or the bed, reach out a paw for enticement, wiggle and pounce. They fell asleep together, Feather wrapped in Skye's arms. They were best friends.

Sadie ignored them in the haughty way only cats do well. One morning in September, I heard a commotion in my yard. Two dogs had jumped the adobe wall and grabbed Skye. By the time I reached him it was too late. He died in my arms, this generous spirit gone much too soon.

Devastated, I rushed him to the vet, against all reason. Feather was bereft. Confused, he waited in all their play places in his pounce position.

If a shadow moved behind a door or with a turn of light he raced to be there. We grieved. I became his protector, his teacher, his pal. He slept in my arms each night.

Now, he is a teenager exploring his world, challenging me. He is Catman. I arrive in Socorro in the midst of an allergic reaction from his scratches. I hole up at Motel 6 for the rest of the afternoon and evening sipping ginger ale, munching soda crackers, watching TV. Finally I fall asleep.

Springtime. The Bosque del Apache. I am in love with this place. Fifty-seven thousand acres devoted to protecting habitat for wildlife.

I walk the Río Viejo Trail. The "old Río Grande" trail winds through an area where refuge staff and volunteers have restored riparian habitat by planting a wide variety of vegetation native to this area: cottonwood, black willow, New Mexico olive and screwbean mesquite.

Animals native to the area, as well as migrating animals, come here to rest and to find food and shelter. I spot a hummingbird basket tucked in the fork of an olive branch. I imagine two eggs, about the size of pinto beans, nestled inside. Or perhaps by now the young have hatched, two babes, no bigger than raisins, clamoring to be fed.

I pause to listen to the song of the Bosque — insects, birds, animals, plants — living the daily business of life. A mule deer rests in the shade of a grand old cottonwood.

Sparrows forage for seeds in the heavy brush. Families of quail zip over ground, parents in the lead, the young racing to keep up. Unseen, Coyote hunts, alert for an unwary bird or rabbit or squirrel.

I walk the river trail remembering the spring floods of my youth. I know humans are small in the face of such great power. Dams, dikes, irrigation channels and other engineering "feats" have tamed most of Earth's grand rivers, giving humans a sense of control. Imagined control at enormous cost. When you stand on the shores of the Columbia River, the Colorado, the Río Grande, you face channeled and toxic waters. Rivers no more. Earth's life. If you visit the dead zone Glen Canyon, and this takes great courage considering it is so deeply painful, you are looking at the Colorado River's coffin.

Before human intervention the Río Grande flooded periodically. When floodwaters receded, sand bars, marshland and mudflats remained, providing fertile ground for seeds to sprout; grasses and shrubs and flowers flourished. Wetlands left behind by the river offered resting places for migrating animals, food and shelter necessary to sustain their journeys. Now, refuge staff and volunteers work as a team to restore the delicate balance of biodiversity essential to the life of an ecosystem.

Springtime. Mid-May. I plan a road trip to Phoenix. Maggie, the Yorkie, will be my traveling companion. Spring cleaning continues. My small car is filled with family treasures for my son, Matthew, my grandson, Jake. My intention is to head out of Albuquerque on I-40 to Flagstaff, a familiar route; but a nudge, a twitch, a pull, and I stay on I-25 toward Socorro. Hmm. I reflect on this turn of events. "Highway 60 to Phoenix. A new route for me." I stop to phone Lori in Magdalena.

It is mid-afternoon when I pull off the highway onto the winding gravel road leading to the B&B. Maggie and I settle into our room. She naps on the bed. I walk outdoors to greet the ranch dogs and horses. My body relaxes, lengthens, remembers what it feels like to breathe.

Later, Lori and I catch up over a glass of wine. I shock myself by asking, "Do you know of a house for rent?"

"Sure," she says, and in minutes I am on the phone with the owner of a sweet little adobe I will soon call home. "Come on over." I find him in the courtyard of his home. He shows me through cool dusky rooms in the beautiful old adobe hacienda where he has lived for seventeen years. Maggie and I meet his dogs. We walk a gravel driveway curving uphill toward the guest house. The two homes sit on thirty acres of hilly desert ground. Within minutes I am writing a check for my first month's rent.

In the morning, it is Gypsy's pleasure I feel as I cruise Highway 60 toward Phoenix. She loves the idea of change, delights in thoughts of new lands to explore.

Springtime. Mother's Day in Phoenix. Matthew hangs the painting of my father on a wall in his den, a place of honor overlooking his new billiard table. We laze over old photograph albums. Jake and I climb a trail in the White Tank Mountains. We visit the World Wildlife Zoo. My master chef son fixes his mother dinner.

I leave for Taos early the next morning, with packing on my mind. Maggie and I drive the long highway home in one twelve-hour day.

Springtime. May 25. Tomorrow morning the movers arrive. The cats and dogs (except Max) and I will drive to Magdalena. Our friend Jeannie will chauffeur Max. This evening, I carry dog blankets to the Laundromat. A streaming afternoon rain shower has moved on, leaving behind delicate sage-freshened air, a vivid twilight, impossibly green hills. I step to the door of the Laundromat to watch a double rainbow spread across the sky. I long to hike the field around the bend, past the park where the rainbow sets down.

Bumper-to-bumper traffic stalls along the main street through town. In the midst of all this tourist congestion, a shiny red convertible decked out with flowers stands out as though alone. A bride and groom sit regally on the rim of the back seat. Both wear white, their jet-black hair glows in the rainbow light. Attendants follow in gleaming New Mexico "low riders," horns blaring.

Viva la Taos! I shout into the wild colorful air.

Listening Deep

The bone tree leans against an adobe wall in front of the house I am renting for the summer. I noticed it first thing, and my heart hummed a quiet shiver of delight. Within moments, my heart handed this information to Gypsy, who, in the dancing shadows of my soul, laughed.

The bone tree, a driftwood sculpture, stands seven feet tall. Wood cradling bone. Each afternoon after a morning of writing, I hunt the bones. I walk golden hills and follow forest roads way back to boulder fields, where wise old faces peer from lichen-covered boulders. I climb into pine forests.

The bone tree grows heavy. Stories grow.

Late one afternoon, I stroll along a shallow arroyo. Off to my left, under a scrub oak, a lengthy rattlesnake rests. The hair on the back of my neck rises. My heart skips a beat, I shudder and turn to leave. Wait! Perhaps she is shedding, a little voice says. Don't you want to take a look? Wariness nudges: *Move it!* And I do.

Wariness, yes. Each day when I hike, a wary self sits on my shoulder, a welcome companion not to be ignored. She is keen to signs of danger. She lives on the side of instinct. Fear of a rattlesnake strike is real fear, not paranoia. Jumped by Cougar. Abducted by Human. Isolated by a sprained ankle. Real fears. Wariness reminds us to stop and pay attention to the energy of a place. Know where you are. Who else is about? Stay alert.

My dogs, my wise hiking companions, alert with the ready power of instinct, hike no more. Arthritis has slowed Hopi Girl; although her heart leaps to hike, her body says no. A weight problem, due to a thyroid condition, keeps Max home. At times I entertain thoughts of a young hiking buddy, but for now I hone my instinctual powers. I listen deeply to regain the living world my body knows. Recovering instinct. It has to do with listening to my animal body, the primal code alert to the energy of a place. It has to do with being attuned to earth's electromagnetic fields. It has to do with the fragile ecology of our planet, with the delicate chemistry in watersheds and rivers and rain forests.

Listening deep, I reassert my instinctual roots through the superficial overlay of a techno/intellectual society. I listen to instinctual layers where the honored bones lay. I catch the enduring rhythm of wild places in my heart.

A recurring dream draws me down to the glowing strata where instinctual power hums and purrs and growls. This dream first came to me when I was a tiny child living in the North Woods of Minnesota. The dream is always the same; when I was very young, it frightened me. I would call out to my parents or run to their bedroom and dive under the covers.

In the dream, a very large cat, a panther, sleeps beside a tiny baby. The crib is small, but somehow the full-grown panther fits himself around the baby, cradles the baby. His long tail curves over the edge of the crib. I think this is what frightened me so as a child. His tail looked like a snake swinging against the railings.

When I awoke from the dream and cried out for her, my mother comforted me. "You have had a wonderful dream," she would murmur. In the morning, at the breakfast table, we looked through picture books of panthers.

Throughout my life I have studied panthers. I know this panther in my body, this instinctual one. I know this holy one who lives on the edge of time. I know now of the old stories of an animal ally attending the baby at the time of birth. I know now of the one who walks with me.

Deep in Earth's heart, Panther walks with slain Buffalo, Wolf, Snow Lion; Panther walks with choked rivers and felled forests. He walks with all wild ones dreaming for Earth, dreaming the way to renew a broken world. Dreaming the way.

My house faces south to the Magdalena Mountains. Above the town, a tumble of rocks on a mountain's eastern face profiles Mary Magdalene, for whom the town and mountains are named. Around the corner I have a unique view of a different Mary Magdalene, one no one else can see. In my view she graces a north-facing rock face. Wait, I explain patiently. Stand right here. Look toward that saddle in the hills, I say. She appears to be sitting for a portrait, her profile graceful; her hair, parted in the center, styled in a bun; her V-neck gown edged in lace.

A pen-and-ink sketch imprinted on the mountainside. This sketch seems to be our secret, Mary Magdalene's and mine.

Legends surround Mary Magdalene. D.H. Lawrence referred to her as the Priestess Isis. Oracle. Jesus referred to her as "the one who knows."

Early Spanish settlers sought protection in the nearby canyons and forests, hiding from Navajo warriors who were said to be superstitious of her presence. (I would love to know the Lady's Navajo name, her Navajo story.) One legend has it that her profile appeared suddenly on the face of the mountain when a group of Spanish soldiers were attacked by Apache.

Her miraculous appearance frightened the Apache attackers and they fled. Another legend claims that certain Native Americans hold this place sacred, as they, in the past, found safety under her wing.

Now, she has cast her spell in our direction.

My animal family is independent here, no fences, no traffic. Hopi Girl scouts her territory as her once grand hiking self. She prowls golden in the sunlight, still the alpha. Max hangs out with our neighbor dogs asserting dominance, at least in his mind. Maggie, always the Yorkie, is our princess.

Lizards race across ground, vanish in a moment. Quail suddenly burst into flight; rabbits disappear under tangled sage. A bobcat may walk through on a given evening, seeking the unwary cat or bird or rabbit, his enticing scent a reminder. Catman studies the ways of the wild. He is no longer my baby; he stands tall, his eyes have deepened. Lean and long-legged, he walks across the ground with the bouncing gait of a young wolf. Sadie, fat and sassy once again, naps on the windowsill.

We fall exhausted onto our pillows each night, windows flung wide to catch the cool desert air. Brilliant night skies seem close enough to touch. Moon peers in as she journeys across the sky. All the birds on Earth must congregate here, whistling and singing in many languages. Quail coo back and forth. Night hawks swoop and dive, scrawling their raspy music overhead. Ravens spin stories. A Mexican brown bat claims the small porch at the front of my house as his own.

Absorbed into the land's silence I share in a whisper of wisdom given off by the barren desert hills, the hot mystical air, the far view…

*Our ability to perceive quality in nature begins, as in art,
with the pretty. It expands through successive
stages of the beautiful to values as
yet uncaptured by language. The quality
of cranes lies, I think, in this higher gamut,
as yet beyond the reach of words.*

ALDO LEOPOLD,
Marshland Elegy, 1949

Enduring Grace

I walk along the Río Grande. Twilight sweeps over the valley. Thousands of cranes fly, dance and feed; their wild presence fills the valley with intimacy. The small streams, the river, the marshes, the cottonwoods, the grand horizon, glow with their presence. I am brought home to the intact natural world I wandered freely as a child, fell in love with, and still crave with all my heart.

Every cell in my being responds to this place. My mind relaxes, empties of chatter, merges with a world of dancing forms, shallow marshes and wild calls carried on the wind.

"What we look at we become," my Swedish grandmother's words remind me. "Once we could become animals, and the animals were us. We saw wisdom in the trees. That is the way we were taught."

What we look at, we become.

At the silent monument for Hiroshima in Japan, a thousand paper cranes dance for peace.

Our broken hearts cry.

Veneration of cranes runs deep in the Orient where the cranes of myth and legend represent immortality. Grace.

What we look at, we become.

On the long drive home, I am reminded of a Japanese legend:

> One day a famous artist was painting, far out in the country. This painter, who lived in a village in Japan, was rich with many comforts. While painting he became thirsty.
>
> When he leaned down to drink at a nearby pool, he saw the reflection of a spectacular bird. He was struck by her beauty and wanted to paint her, but when he looked up the bird was gone. He walked for many days in search of her. Wherever he went, he described the bird and people said, "Yes, the bird was just here roosting near the lake," or "Yes, it just passed over my hut and is now resting far out on an island in the middle of the lake." People warned him, "The lake is cold and deep; it is too treacherous a journey across the lake for a man like you."

For a time the painter returned to his village. His friends praised his work, yet to him his paintings were empty. He explained to his friends that he had caught a glimpse of truth, and he could not paint unless he found it again. He sold his house and his paintings and started back to the lake. He begged a fisherman to sell him his boat. He rowed out onto the lake. The cold breath of winter chilled the air; ferocious winds swirled over the lake. His boat capsized in the icy water. Almost frozen, he swam toward the island and managed to reach the shore. His strength was spent.

Before him, he saw a flock of great birds. The birds moved toward him in the cool mists. They were preparing to fly to a warmer climate. When they spread their powerful wings and flew off, the sky was filled with their music.

Then, the painter understood. Truth is impossible to capture, for it lives freely, in wild hearts. "At least I know this," he whispered. "It is enough." As he sat quietly, watching the birds fly from the island, large wings appeared at his sides, feathers warmed his body. Far above the lake, the birds called, and he echoed their call. His great wings carried him far above the water, through the mists, to join his brothers.*

*Story borrowed from Claude Clément, *The Painter and the Wild Swans*.

The Bone Tree

July. Doors and windows open wide to greet the sweet morning air and birdsong. The dogs patrol their boundaries, sending greetings across the way to Annie and Barclay. Sadie relaxes on a sunny window ledge. Catman naps, recovering from a night out.

July is my birthday month. July was also my father's and my Irish grandfather's birthday month. Often, we celebrated together when I was a child. My mother, grandmother and the aunts baked angel-food cakes, chocolate cakes and pies. Food preparation occupied all available counter space in our kitchen. I chopped carrots, listened in on conversations, scooped fingers full of thick fudge frosting from mixing bowls. The tantalizing heat of ham, homemade bread and desserts drifted through the house.

Outdoors, hamburgers sizzled on the grill. Small children played on the lawn. Grown-ups lounged on lawn chairs, smoking and visiting. Long wooden picnic tables covered with red-checked oilcloth held relish trays, paper plates, cups, covered casseroles, jam. In time, the women and the uncles carried platters of ham, potato salad, jugs of lemonade and tins of fresh homemade hamburger buns from the kitchen to fill the tables. At last, with grand tribute, songs were sung and the cakes were carried out. Lighted candles crowned each cake. Birthday wishes floated on summer breezes over trees toward that place where wishes go.

July. I raise the flag to celebrate Independence Day and to honor birthdays past and present. For every national holiday and each special occasion in our family, my dad raised the flag.

I was a toddler when I first stood with him and watched as he hooked the flag to ropes on the flag pole. I watched him raise the flag to wind, sky and clouds. This was magical for me. Important. The flag snapped. "There She is." Dad would say. He would give a little skip, a courtly bow.

When I grew older, Dad taught me to fold the flag properly, to carry it as you would a prayer. From my Dad I learned my country's history.

My love for our nation's flag is organic. Dad raised the flag on our birthdays, and when my babies were born. He raised the flag for our homecomings. He raised the flag in celebration of life and to honor the dead. He raised the flag to honor his brother, our Uncle Abe. He raised the flag to honor our country. In ceremony.

My Dad hunted. I learned to shoot, to care for a gun. We ate the venison or pheasant or quail. We walked, a rifle held in the crook of an arm. We walked a bright fall day though woods so beautiful your heart would break, walking the colors, the scents.

I remember an early morning in autumn. My dad —
dressed in red flannel shirt, a leather vest, a heavy wool Pen-
dleton jacket and Timberland boots — was loading his small
truck, preparing to meet his friends at their hunting camp.
Perhaps I was eleven years old. I don't like this, I told him. It
isn't fair. The deer have no guns. He answered with the stock
answer of a hunter. "We keep the population down. Otherwise
the herd starves."

My dad was not one to display a trophy head on the wall.
In fact, not long after this time, in my memory, he stopped
hunting. I do not believe it had anything to do with my plea. I
believe he had a bad experience. Lost on an island off the coast
of Canada, he spent a cold night alone in bear country, his
back against a tree.

Stories of the ancestors. Family stories. Stories from the
road. Stories, caught in the night, rumbling about in my uncon-
scious, to be hunkered down with over coffee in the morning,
or at 2 a.m., when I can't sleep. Some stories, I have imagined or
dreamed to life. Most I have found in the bones, in the organic
matter of earth, in the organic matter of my body.

Stories are there wherever I am. Waiting to be known. If
I settle my mind to listen, they are there in the shadows of my
heart. Stories to bring me home.

The bone tree outside my door hisses, sings, hums,
growls, roars and howls stories.

Querencia

When I was ten years old I spent several weeks in late August at my grandparents' farm. I was there to help Grandma with chores, which included gathering vegetables from the garden, filling lunch buckets for the men, sweeping floors, washing dishes, running and fetching.

August was harvest time, the busiest time of the year on the farm. Grandpa hired extra field hands to bring in the grain. Grandma kept the household running smoothly.

Some days I rode the grain truck to Lankin with Leon. We waited in a long line of trucks with other farmers hauling grain to the granary. Here the grain was weighed and sold, separated from the chaff and stored in silos. The men stood outside their trucks, one arm resting on the window sill of the open driver's door, catching up on news of their neighbors, talking prices, family. The sharp smell of grain hung in the air. The sky was blue, cloudless, the grain golden. I sat in the truck enjoying being part of the amiable atmosphere, the work.

Everything happened in Lankin. We bought groceries here, supplies for the farm, gas for the trucks. The grocery store was also a hardware store, a fabric store and a café. The men sat around on benches and barrels, drinking coffee, smoking, spinning tales. Everyone knew Leon and me. "Well, well, Emil's granddaughter. How do you do?" And they would shake my hand, remarking on my strong grip. "Good strong girl."

Farmers—men in denim coveralls, plaid shirts, jackets, billed caps, dusty work boots; men who smelled of grain, sweat and pipe tobacco. Solid men. I burst with pride at their attention. Yes, I was strong, I thought. Strong like Grandma. Just that morning I had watched her chop the head off a chicken with one strike of the ax.

Leon was my buddy. He was Mexican. His English was marginal, yet we communicated beautifully. He talked and I listened. For as long as I could remember he had worked the harvest with my grandfather. He had cradled me when I was a baby.

On our drives to town, I listened to his stories of Mexico, his family, his children. I could not imagine such a place. He also played the harmonica—a wonder to me, a tone-deaf kid born into a nonmusical family.

That year I developed a particular fascination with the yard bull, Old Mick. Mick's domain was a sturdily fenced enclosure behind the barn. Whenever I had free time, I sat on the top rail of the wooden fence watching him. He snorted, and pawed the ground raising dust. I worried that he was lonely and pestered Grandpa endlessly. "This is how it is for Old Mick," was his answer. Still I fretted. I decided I would become Old Mick's friend. Secretly I hauled carrots, lettuce, rutabagas, potatoes from the garden and dumped the vegetables through the railings of his pen.

One day I sat perched on the top rail. Would he eat from my hand? I pondered. I leaned over holding out a carrot. Come here, Mick, I called. I lost my balance and fell head first into the bull pen. I landed on my stomach inches from Mick's sharp hooves. I could not breathe, or call for help. From somewhere, I heard Leon yelling in Spanish. Where did he come from? I wondered.

I watched Mick trot, head down, toward the far corner of his pen. Leon jumped the fence and helped me to my feet. Without a word he opened the gate and we walked through. Quietly he shut the gate. I burst into tears. Later, during dinner, I heard Leon telling the men. "Cheri (his name for me) fell to ground. Old Mick bolted for his querencia." I was in the kitchen with Grandma. She had just handed me a platter of the aforementioned chicken to carry into the dining room. I stopped in the doorway to listen. Querencia.

Querencia, I whispered. The word caught my attention.

I set the platter on the table. "Querencia, Leon, what does it mean?" No one at the table could translate.

Returning to the kitchen I asked Grandma. "Safe place," she told me. "It means safe place." She looked straight at me and said sternly. "Old Mick went to his safe place. Don't bother him anymore."

*What mysterious code guides us
inevitably into our original and unforeseeable destiny?*

Regeneration

Seven years ago, fire ravaged thousands of acres of this forest.
Today I follow a well-worn elk trail to the crest of a hill overlooking a charred landscape, an ethereal world of blackened
lodgepole pines, blue spruce, oak. Beautiful in their starkness.
I step around or crawl over tangled sculptures of fallen tree
trunks. I breathe deep silence. Vital energy. Earth energy.
Animal energy.

Wildness pads through my body.

I walk downslope toward sparkling light. A creek wends
her way through tall grasses. My dogs sink belly deep into the
water. A copper-colored butterfly rests on a flowering bush. A
chickadee sings. A concert of insects tune up. A wren perches
at the tip of a willow. While I watch, she hops down branch
by branch until she reaches water to take a sip. I rest on a soft
muddy island in the middle of the stream. I cover myself with
mud and doze.

I dream Raven and all that Raven knows. The mud hardens and shrinks. Beneath the mud my body tightens, cracks open, turns to dust, and washes downstream.

When I awake, I watch from a rocky ledge as a herd of elk graze in a faraway meadow. For as far as I can see, young pine trees sprout, green and vibrant, burst forth from seeds hibernating underground and heated by a fire seven years gone. Nearby, a gleaming reddish gold stump spills wood dust onto the ground, replenishing the soil. A barrel cactus sports a single cardinal red flower. Fields of wildflowers put on a show, all delicate and subtle. Pure beauty mirrors the heavens and all of the subtleties we don't know.

I face East and raise my arms in prayer. Some say it is from the East that we receive the dream, the inspiration. Some say dreams for Earth ride East Wind's soft song.

I face West, home to canyon, mountain and desert. I offer prayers to Earth, who supports my walk. I face North where wolf calls, defining the sanctuary of his home.

I turn to face South. I ask to define my power, my heart's vision.

* * *

A black and gold king snake rests just below the rocky ledge where I stand. I crouch for a better look. Long minutes pass. I worry she may be dead. She is so still. I crawl slowly down over the rocks as close as I dare. I don't wish to frighten her. My dogs watch from the ledge above. I hold my breath. I see her tongue flicker in and out. Quietly I back away. The dogs and I take up our watch. A long time later she glides toward an underground place…and disappears.

* * *

I build a small fire pit. Twigs of sage and dry pinecones burn. The haunting aroma of sage and wood smoke fill the air.

I dream serpent. From the base of my spine, from a place deep within, serpent uncoils. She weaves her magic, reaches into my heart, ignites fire. Behind my eyes she touches vision opening to a timeless universe. The Ancestors rumble in my blood. My body comes to life, dances waves of fluid power. Dust rises.

I drop onto the hot sand to follow snake's winding path, dreaming her rhythm.

* * *

Twilight touches the land. I walk toward a forest untouched by fire. Gold light plays through pine branches. Pine scents the air. Layers of pine needles carpet the ground. Spirit friends rustle around me, their presence so strong I turn to look. They nestle near my shoulders. Friendly old voices come to call. I am reminded of my father's wisdom. "Become your own woman," expressing a wisdom unusual for the time, or even now. I, of course, shrugged my shoulders. He could have been speaking a foreign language for all the attention I paid. Only now do I understand the journey inward. The place of integrity.

A great rush of joy throws me to the ground, to a fragrant bed of pine. Flowing as serpent I slip into my quiet den. I rest here until dark. Remembering. Accepting the woman that I am. Taking her with me when I leave.

The Canyon Trail

The canyon trail, where time is measured in the slow shedding of a snake skin.

Yesterday I walked a sandy trail crisscrossed by Snake. She left her mark curved deep in soft sand. A red-tail hawk circled gracefully overhead, dropped a feather as a prayer. I looked to the darkening sky and watched the feather spiral to earth, caught by a snag on the shore of a muddy marsh, the snag where Owl waits at midnight for Rabbit. Blue-black thunderclouds rumbled past distant hills. Lightning cut a slash to the ground. Coyote skipped playfully from behind a stand of golden cottonwood, glanced in my direction, turned slowly to slip back into the shadows. A yellow-footed lizard waited patiently under a desert willow for that first drop of rain to fall.

It was an ordinary day on the Canyon Trail.

I hike this sweet little meander summer and winter. Some mornings I leave my home at dawn, when the air feels cool as silk. Light breaks over the eastern horizon as if for the first time, and thousands of snow geese lift off ponds in one swift motion. All noise and grace.

Words always fall short of wildness. It is a bloody risk to write of vulnerability…the vulnerability of a wild place…where wisdom lives in Falcon's swoop, in the carefully constructed den of Rock Wren, in the social life of Coyote, in the silence following Hawk's screee. In the ancient soul of Crane.

I like to walk alone. I go for the roam, the opportunity to slow down, to know silence. I hike to feel the energy of a place, to touch the stories. Stories told by the creatures who live here. Stories written in the rocks. Stories told in geologic time, in myriad folds and crevices shaped by wind and water. Stories told in the magnetic pull of eroded sculptures, in the mystical grottos smoothed by time, passageways into unseen worlds where mythology and geology conspire. The rocks know I do not matter. They care nothing for those of us who wander here.

They offer gifts of humility.

The soft sandy path I follow winds through a field of waist-high desert plants, now brown and dormant.

A world of tracks dance over the ground, marking the busy nightlife of creatures who pounce, leap, hop, walk, slither and crawl. I imagine the action of survival. A deer mouse munches juniper seeds outside his burrow, his bright eyes watchful. A beetle kicks up a mound of sand to hide his tiny shelter. Coyote stalks Rabbit. Pounces. Throws him in the air just for practice. Rattlesnake coils. Tail shakes. Strike! Fox catches every movement from the shelter of his cozy den. Tortoise waits. Patience, the rhythm of the desert.

If you take this walk, you may spot large round pug prints pressed deep in the sand. If you are particularly observant you may notice that the tracks follow a trail pounded into the ground by mule deer. It is unlikely you will see the grand cougar. Not because they aren't here: they are, a precious few of them. The big cat is primarily nocturnal and exceedingly shy. Wisely, Cougar is wary. Human smells of danger.

Bobcats also find this canyon to their liking. They prowl the high rocky cliffs as ghostlike in their movements as their larger cousins.

Under a stone overhang in the soft white sand, delicate, perfect four-toed tracks and a swipe of tail mark the working life of a kangaroo rat.

If you are very quiet, you may catch sight of Coyote digging for rodents. Rodents are plentiful here, easy prey not just for Coyote and other four-footed predators but for soaring canyon dwellers, too. A variety of raptors, eagles, falcons and that most persistent and successful airborne pursuer of small nocturnal creatures, the great horned owl, find a choice smorgasbord on which to feed in this desert landscape. At least one great horned owl makes this canyon home. I've watched his great silent self swoop through a narrow canyon to become invisible in the next moment. Even more numerous than their rodent neighbors and prey are the reptiles whose comings and goings are often overlooked. They are everywhere, sunning on rocks and in the eroded crevices where they make their homes. They are everywhere, watching you.

Today, a vivid blue sky discloses a show of half moon. I straggle off toward a mysterious side canyon. A sunny wall beckons. I lean into sunbaked rock and close my eyes. Hours pass. Who knows how many? Mindless chatter melts away. A soft breeze lifts self-importance by the shirttail, flings it into the air to be snagged by Raven. I bake in the heat, dreaming the life of lizards. Perfectly in place. Across the way, afternoon sun back-lights the high ridge. A flame of light casts a four-wing saltbush in silver. Moments later, wired by the sun gods, the whole crag-gy ridge of vegetation ignites. Such beauty cannot be written.

A flute's mellow notes break through my reverie. Koko-pelli beckons. Ahhh, Kokopelli, I grin, and out of curiosity bow to his compelling call. Kokopelli turns out to be an ordinary guy (I think) testing the acoustics in this natural amphitheater. The flute's haunting melody echoes off the canyon walls.

Kokopelli's friend Diane holds a snake shed, fragile as a whisper. "I found this right here." She gestures to the ground beneath a clump of sage. She holds the translucent snakeskin gently curved in her arms; they both shimmer in the light. So beautiful, I say, the shedding of the skin. "All the time." Diane smiles. "All the time."

The three of us stand together to marvel at the history in the rocks. We point to layers telling of shifts and rumbles in Earth time. We trace delicate lines etched in the hardened dunes, admire the sensuous shape and texture of sandstone walls. We peer cautiously into rock crevices high above ground, where pack-rat middens grow large, their urine-cemented piles of plant material, bones and other matter thousands of years old. One could spend a lifetime working out pack-rat-midden stories from before the time of the Piro Indians and beyond. Fresh scat, seeds, sticks, pebbles and a few shiny objects offer evidence of present-day use by pack-rat descendants. "I'll just bet thousands of years from now, a bit of blue plastic found in a pack-rat midden will be studied, scanned, and puzzled over." Kokopelli muses.

When you walk the Canyon Trail you may notice tiny round holes scattered across the face of the rock walls. The solitary wasp drills these holes, paralyzes a spider, places Spider in the opening, and lays her lone egg on top of Spider. Although the spider is paralyzed, it is alive: fresh food for the baby wasp to eat when the egg hatches.

I climb the steep trail to stand at the top of the mesa. Behind me, the sun drops over the Chupadera Mountains. To the east for as far and wide as I can see, distance extends. From this vantage, I could mention snow geese rising in great flashes of brilliant light over marshland where only raucous bird voices rule. I could mention sandhill cranes, how their primal energy fills my soul. I could mention our once-grand río, her wild meander tamed. I could mention the lone snag where Eagle perches, watching for his prey. I could mention how the Little San Pasqual Mountains, a small range composed of layers of Paleozoic rock, glow crimson set off by blood red skies; and beyond, where lightning cracks the sky open and great painted cliffs rise as if from the sea.

I could mention a young bobcat running full out across the mesa toward me as though in play. His golden eyes stare me down, questioning my place.

Later, much later, Coyote calls. Owl wakes. Mountains sharpen to black. Ponds mirror the light of a cold blue moon. Some desert dwellers gather to dream. Others prowl. I walk home to the hum of desert life as night falls. I walk in the tracks of Turtle and Mouse, Lizard, Rabbit and Snake. Deer. Bobcat. Mountain Lion. I walk in the tracks of all those who have gone before.

Coyote calls. All is quiet. All is mystery.

If You Go to the Mountain
Take Only a Little of Yourself

I follow a stream leading into the highest ridges of the Sangre de Cristos. Tiny rivulets of water sound beneath ice crystals, carrying songs of renewal, birth and age. Lichen-covered boulders shoulder the stream banks, attentive to all who pass; shaped and textured by water, mud, fire and time, their sturdy old spirits breathe life from the center of the Earth. Fish and insects and plants embedded in each massive, rough, granite body live on from a time when earth and shallow oceans tumbled, shifted, shattered, formed and dried. I lean in, nose to stone, to breathe the musty scent of humus, fog-shrouded sloughs, and saltwater. Images of Earth form in my mind as a kaleidoscope of molten rumblings, dense clouded skies, sea creatures bellowing in lightning-blasted waters, prehistoric beasts. I place my hands to feel a drum-like pulse. My fingertips scan winged edges of white shell, the bumpy structure of pebbles. I savor subtle diversities of color — red, green, black, white and gray.

Stepping back, I stare at the complex map before me, of life caught by faces etched in stone. Turtles, lizards, dinosaurs — great old beings from swampy seas of long ago remind me that I live in a slip of time. Wending their way through millenniums, these tranquil old seers know the true turning of history and what is to come.

Where I walk today, young Fir and Spruce perhaps a foot high stand lush and green, shimmering in the stillness of this sunlit morning. Groves of Aspen, ethereal in early-morning light, cradle baby shoots under a blanket of moldering leaves. A single tree's root structure may push hundreds of quaking seedlings above ground — tough resilient sprouts fired in silt and clay and lime. Home to generations, an aspen grove's root system expands outward beneath the soil, in community with mountain, light, moisture, and creatures winged and furred and scaled.

The mountain is filled with stories — birth and love stories, wizard poetry, stories of truths encountered, stories of beauty and passion and loss, stories of fear, sadness and longing.

If you go to the mountain let the mountain take you in — to the place inside where you feel how it all flows together. For this is who you are.

Far up the mountain in the tundra, hidden beneath a certain overhang of rocks, near where cougar rests his bones, lives a spring, the birthplace of rivers. The climb to the headwaters is difficult and long. I want to be here, in this secret place where water bubbles up catching light, returning again to darkness. I practice my longing here, my dreams. Coyote comes by with

Wind to show me pages from their story...a story of forever. Cougar comes by with her cub to show me pages from their story of boundless grace, invisibility and terror. Rabbit hops by carrying his pages proudly. He is too shy to share.

Water comes by with Light to show me pages sparkling with tears, pages wet with tears of River and Wolf and Grizzly, Eagle and Whooping Crane. Pages filled with dreams of oceans, sun and rain, snow and ice and clouds. Prairie Dog comes by carrying pages containing stories of community, of the subterranean world of roots and soil, of water and rock, of fellows who tunnel and aerate so soil breathes moisture, calling down the rain.

All of nature sends the gift of interconnection. Our genetic coding reminds us we are connected hand and foot, heart and soul, to a destiny unfolding.

In geological terms Earth's surface is called fluff. Humanity has laid superficial worlds onto Earth's surface, worlds we superimpose over reality, imagine as real. It is easy to lose our way here, become captive, forget the brightness of silence, water, air and earth. Serious homage is given to distraction — the frenzy, the insecurity, the fractured busyness, the gadgets, the noise. Easy to get lost here. When we bury our hearts and souls in the surface worlds of cement, technology, entertainment and being cool, how do we find the wild place within? How do we know the sightings of the moon, the patterns of the stars, the heart-raw awe of sunset and dawn, the communication of other species?

Beneath the fluff, Earth is alive with beginnings. Patterns for creation are found in a labyrinth of tunnels where Earth dreams a most delicate dream. Powerful stories live in the elemental world of darkness. A sacred place remaking future. All wild nature remembers how it is to be here.

My footprints fade into the gravely trail I follow toward my home in the valley. Rumpled Earth reminds me I walk again through the sleeping place of bears. The Earth pulses with the steady rhythm of their breath.

I stop to feel the deepening music flowing out of the ground. My feet shuffle, raising dust. My body shifts and turns, I bow down a bit, my shoulders expand, my arms spread out to the side. I beat my palms against my thighs. I lift my feet to circle. Circling in and out, I stomp and twist and shimmy. I dance while tears fall. I dance, and the sweat of the dance is like beads of quicksilver on my body. I remember the importance of gesture. I dance as a gesture, just to let Bear know I know his place is here, grounded in the center of miracles. All the lifeblood of the world is here!

Water Catches Light

*Coming home to the perfect
elsewhere.*

Coming Home

Where I walk, swirling waves roll out of a labyrinth of canyons. Coursing down the mountain, on its raucous way toward the far beyond, río's lusty beat sweet talks me to sit awhile. I find a patch of cool ground under a grove of cottonwoods, where sunlight filters through. The trees glow in a shadowy way, rustling softly, showing off the perfection of their heart-shaped leaves. A file of Canada Geese sails by dipping low, skimming gracefully over the water. Skyscraper chimneys rise out of a rosy sandstone pyramid on the opposite shore. I pull my sketch pad out of my pack — loving what is unbroken, rough, wild. I stretch full out enjoying a sultry pleasure. Invisible and rowdy and present. Above, beyond the lacy tree branches the sky moves at a rather dizzying pace. Infinite.

Later in the day I follow a rough trail leading to an unknown place in a long valley where the river meanders slow and quiet in a most beautiful way. I note tracks of birds and tiny rodents; tracks of Bear and Bobcat, Coyote, Fox, Deer, Raccoon — each a reflection, a flash of light birthed out of River's rugged heart. Lynx come down from the highest peaks. Blue heron perch in cottonwood trees. Camouflaged by mud and leaves, grandaddy frogs affect the life of stones. A feast of insects whirl overhead, lighting up the air with iridescent wings. At night I sleep on the soft-sand shore, burrowing my body down, linked to, imprinted by River's fluid motion, surrendering, one body to another. Fog rises out of the river tinged with sparkles of silver star. My favorite kind of time. Anything is possible.

I dream a nest made of good-sized sticks woven together in a sturdy yet tangled way. The whole nest is large and deep. The basket is round and comfortable looking. Before my eyes a very young eaglet is dropped into the nest. The baby is covered in white feathery down. A few round objects are set around in the nest...eggs, perhaps?

I wake, wondering how will I care for this young one... feed and nourish such an other creature. At the center of things, straight from the womb, this little eaglet carries a fierce hope. My training says Earth dreams through us...we draw our energy, authenticity, from Earth.

Coming home, holding this baby dear, as an ally, as valuable ground, allows me an astonishing chance to...settle in...to be responsive to her needs, to the fierce hope she carries.

King of the skies, an eagle is magnificence in flight. Grace. Two species are widespread in North America: golden eagle and bald eagle. Distinguished by white feathered heads, tails, and undertail coverts, dark feathered bodies, yellowish beaks, and narrow dark eye-lines, adult bald eagles, as with all raptors, hunt by the strength of their eyes, their focused attention.

Curved horn-colored beaks with dark tips characterize a golden eagle's aristocratic face. Golden hackles highlight his numinous glow. A tawny feathered bar reaches across the length of each dark wing. A golden's legs are feathered to their toes, tipped in amber light.

Eagles are territorial, claiming a wide-open landscape, building nests in cliffs, trees, or rocky ledges, away from other predators. Soaring over mountains, valleys, meadows, large bodies of water—catching thermals, swooping, gliding—eagles bear infinite mystery in their great bodies, a genetic coding tuned to the natural order of life. Eagles are age-old partici-pants in nurturing creation.

Each parent hunts for its young. Dropping out of the sky, wings upturned, talons raised, grasping prey—at times feeding right there on the ground or lifting off, heading for the nest. I have watched an eagle walking in tall grass meadows scouting gophers, mice, snakes. The eaglet in my dream is very young, still wearing his/her down.

Alert and hungry. Dependent on care.

Coming home to taste this spectacular valley in my own way: what is there here? A world of stories. Rain moving in and out of shadowy hills through thunderclouds. Sunrise in muted shades of gold and crimson. Migrating flocks of cranes guided by memory of watershed and river. Hidden lakes, shimmering streams. Granite boulders holding shapes of sea creatures. Red rock hoodoos lifting out of the ground as monsters. Miles of valley encircled by mountains, space to roam, or stay still. What is there here? Bear. Bobcat. Coyote. All sorts of wildlife in motion. A place where I forgive myself for times I didn't take care, for the intensity of my path.

Coming home where life is uncontrived, my routine falls into place. I have relocated once again to a place I've known before. My hidden strange uncertainty is okay here rambling about, trusting enough to feel safe, trusting my feral invisibility, claiming my territory. Coming home.

Some mornings, mist floats over the valley, turns to snow in the afternoon. This evening, snow falls fat and heavy. Dense dark clouds shadow the Sangre de Cristos. A strip of twilight illuminates the river's edge. A pair of yellow eyes glance in my window. Coyote walks past, fading into the murky blue dusk, heading home. Leaving paw prints on the path.

Quiet. A pair of ravens settle in among the branches of a pine tree near the ditch. Huge wet snowflakes drift straight down, launching me out the door to walk through perfect prisms of cold white light.

Magic.

Siste Viator! (Pause, Traveler!)

In the predawn hours, I slip into warm clothes to walk outdoors with my little dog Coco. I carry a small cup of coffee and plod along behind her. A sheen of light edges over the Sangre de Cristo Range. Sunrise illuminates the silken threads of a giant spider web woven through the uppermost leafless branches of a cottonwood tree. A heart-shaped leaf, just one, rests on waves of snow-covered ground beneath the tree, exquisitely in place. A bald eagle perches on a branch in a nearby grove of cottonwoods.

My very early mornings are like this. Coco entices me out of a warm bed. Leashed together we walk the streets and alleyways of this tiny town in the heart of the San Luis Valley. Coco, master of "the pause" stops frequently to sniff and stare, checking out her surroundings, the age-old practice of the pause called down from her terrier genes.

We both pause. I, so often caught in thought, am surprised when I return to the luminous world, awake. Just there, right before my eyes, a ferruginous hawk in the pasture tears into his morning meal. Our silent morning meander brings us too close. Suddenly we are there. He turns to glare. Majestic. All grace and beauty, luxuriously feathered in brown and shining white.

Again, as always when I encounter a wild creature, I am stilled by their astounding presence. In natural surroundings, animals carry an intrinsic belonging. An energy of place. "Important thought" does not hinder their mindful daily routine. An animal's actions are focused, unselfconscious, elemental. An animal moves from his whole body, synchronized, totally present. Aware.

"What is smart is our bodies, our breath," writes Natalie Goldberg in *Wild Mind.* Who are we really? I wonder. Animal... anima...soul? Or are we always to be caught in performance, dressed for the occasion? Coifed, fashioned and caged? Identity intact? Who are we really? How is it to be truly present?

My grandmother would say, *"The miracle is to walk the Earth,"* as would the old Zen masters. And so it is.

My big dogs Charley and Little Bud take me on a turn into the far view. One of our favorite places is Russell Lakes, a Natural National Landmark just outside of town, a closed basin of wetlands fed by underground aquifers. We run unleashed across the mesa, where wetlands and marsh grasses reflect all the mystery there is, where calls of geese and sandhill cranes are the only sounds. We scout out secret places, pausing here and there. A raised wooden deck overlooks the distant landscape. Coyote scat claims territory on the edge of the deck. Coyote, a fine opportunist, elicits our praise; we stand on the deck to yip and howl for a place still rambunctious enough to house Coyote's clan. My dogs and I trace Coyote's tracks, iconic traveler that he is, into the blue light of the San Luis Valley.

* * *

Spring arrived early this year after a long cold winter. Snowpack lies deep on mountain peaks, promising a good run-off for our parched ground. The call of sandhill cranes overhead is an unmistakable sign of renewal. Of the Rocky Mountain population of sandhill cranes, 95 percent travel through the San Luis Valley in spring and fall along the Río Grande corridor as did their ancestors before them.

Monte Vista National Wildlife Refuge in Southern Colorado provides a much-needed rest stop on their long migration from winter sanctuaries in New Mexico toward their northern nesting grounds in the Greater Yellowstone Ecosystem and beyond.

This refuge in the gray misty light emits a mythic feel. It simply glows with energy. I am the only person here today in the midst of a landscape both remote and nurturing, an inter-mountain valley surrounded by the Sangre de Cristo Range to the east and the San Juans to the west. Mt. Blanca, a standout, shows off her luscious shimmering snowfields.

Water on the Monte Vista Refuge follows a gentle almost flat slope of valley floor, creating a mosaic of meadow and shallow marshland. Cattails and sedge grass provide a dense cover for nesting ducks and water birds. The northern harrier builds her nest on the soft cover of marsh grass.

Refuge water is gravity fed from one wetland to another; or, during dry times, water is pumped from deep aquifers by refuge staff. Predators and prey alike live and work here as nature intended.

The refuge in the spring rings with the calls of sandhill cranes. Groups of cranes lift off or touch down, long legs extended, each gracious body finding a place in the ponds or in flight among their fellows. A love song in sound and motion. Thousands of cranes feed and call and dance with all the power, energy, and beauty carved in their ancient souls; their large bodies and wingspans evoke visions of prehistoric marshes and creatures long gone. I watch from a distance in wonder at the miracle of standing in the presence of all this *life*.

*"…a living community of interrelations
more complex than the most brilliant among us
has the power to conceive."*

WILLIAM DEBUYS
The Walk

Water Catches Light

To understand a river's ecology, begin with care and time. It takes time for intimacy to grow; it takes time to step outside ourselves to realize we are but a tiny part of the language and mystery and beauty of the river's story.

In the rhythm of rivers, we touch a powerful mystery. Their wild landscape sweeps into our cells as breath. Transparent as breath. It is no longer important or possible to hold a pose. We surrender to love, a complicated story, and yet we pursue. The river takes a firm hold. Somehow our hidden strange uncertainty, our soul's longing, hauls us to the shore again and again. We pause long to listen to River's strong meandering voice, to become a part of her forceful presence.

Blue light and dark canyons house creatures of blinding complexity. Unforgettable rhythms linger and tantalize. We dance to a beat deep down. River's music echoes across the hills and canyons, thumping out the old songs. Reminding us that we are working on a story, delicate and changing. Our story depends on whether we find the time to uncover our mystical core, the place inside where we are alive enough, raw enough, to take in the rhythm of wild rivers; the mystique of raindrop and cloud and ocean; the splendid architectural genius of a swallow's cliffside mud basket; the caretaking in the tiny woven basket of a hummingbird; the migration flyways of sandhill cranes; the intricacy of a bear's sturdy lair, ceiling braced by logs, sleeping shelf softened by pine boughs. All on the edge of just surviving. And yet our world still holds such wondrous creations.

Several years ago I embarked on a journey to follow the Río Grande from Creede, Colorado, to its headwaters at Stony Pass in the San Juan Range of the Rocky Mountains. I would then backtrack downstream into New Mexico and Texas.

Spring snowmelt begins slowly in the high tundra of the Rocky Mountains. Above tree line at an elevation of 13,821 feet, winter storms encase mountain peaks in ice and snow. Trickles of water flow from craggy peaks; water pure enough to drink seeps underground to bubble up out of the Earth, becoming streams, flowing together, to form the headwaters of the Río Grande.

The upper Río Grande Watershed includes almost two million acres of forest on the eastern slope of the Continental Divide in Colorado. A wide variety of ecological terrains — volcanic and glacial, mountainous, steep canyons (mostly roadless or traversed by rough, pocked jeep trails) — are challenging indeed for the hiker.

Throughout history this extraordinary landscape of extreme beauty and harshness provided shelter, food and spiritual meaning to travelers and residents alike. In present time, the river and its watershed are severely compromised. Wildness still exists in places. Raptors roost in cliffs above the river, soaring over the mesa's sagebrush plains and native grasslands to hunt. Large and small mammals, snakes and amphibians are plentiful, particularly upstream in the Río Grande National Forest and in the 242,555 thousand acres that compose the Río Grande del Norte National Monument in Northern New Mexico.

The monument, established to protect an iconic landscape, spans southward from the borderlands of Colorado and New Mexico to just north of Pilar and from the Río de los Pinos State Wildlife area in the far northwest to the easternmost point of Guadalupe Mountain northwest of Questa, New Mexico. Pine and piñon forests, canyons and meadows of wildflowers contain a cauldron of life. Raptors, deer, antelope, fox, coyote, bighorn sheep, cutthroat trout, elk, bear, mountain lion, and countless small species essential to an integral ecosystem call this place home.

The Río Grande Gorge, part of the Central Migratory Flyway, essential to the survival of many migratory species, opens on the plains at the western edge of Ute Mountain. Established in 2013, portions of the monument are already threatened. A large-scale power grid, proposed by Tri-State Generation and Transmission, will run straight through Ute Mountain if approved. Military flyovers from both Cannon and Kirtland Air Force bases severely impact the landscape with their voluminous noise.

The tragedy is, as always, the terrible intrusion. Of us. How we view our world, what we allow to be important, what we ignore, settles in our bodies. Our sorrow, a tension behind the eyes, or deep in the belly, is barely noticeable because it has always been there, shuttered, held off, caught in our breath, our hesitancy, our wars, our desperate need to numb ourselves with chemicals. In *River Notes*, Barry Lopez shares his personal sorrow, sorrow acknowledged as a soul's need for truth: "You will know a loss of guile and that the journey has begun."

* * *

Once upon a time, when the river was wild, beaver colonies thrived in partnership with the river, important to the river's story. The placement of their lodges influenced hydrology — moderating the river's flow, spreading water, creating marshland, creating habitat. If you are lucky enough to spend a day or longer with this industrious creature, you are offered a rare glimpse into a river's complex ecology, where roots grow deep and the substance of life is rich, timeless in the feel of a place. Just at twilight, if you are quiet and patient, you may watch a stir of creatures meet at the water's edge: a rustle, a soft padding, delicate shadows tread well-worn dirt paths, untouched by ignorance or greed.

* * *

Canada geese, sandhill cranes, raptors, herons, American avocets, and songbirds wing their way southward following the río's pathway toward winter sanctuaries like the Bosque del Apache NWR, and the Río Grande Nature Center in New Mexico. When the river ran free of dams and human encroachment, wetlands and riparian vegetation were plentiful along the river, providing rest stops, shelter and food for migrating and resident animals. In our modern times, the river and wildlife are diminished by drought, development, chemicals, erosion.

Wildlife depends on us to restore and conserve habitat.

The mythic rhythm of the Río Grande generates passion, a sense of responsibility. In Southern Colorado, three unique National Wildlife Refuges — Monte Vista, Alamosa, and the Baca — are essential havens for migrating and residential species. Sandhill cranes, as well as many other species, find rest in these protective life-giving wetlands. Dedicated groups of individuals and organizations work tirelessly for the river. Mike Gibson points out: "Restoration of the river understands what the river has done historically. Partnership is the key, learning from the river." Greg Higel, a rancher west of Alamosa, Colorado, recalls: "As I grow older, I understand the vitality of the Río Grande Watershed; wildlife and human needs are intertwined." The Higel Conservation Easement is a testament to his commitment.

∗ ∗ ∗

I drive south on a dirt road, then off on another dirt road west, into a world behind time. I cross invisible borders to a primeval landscape. The blue hills across the wide mesa pull me inside to a place where all my longings converge. I stand on this mesa, on this grand open landscape. A feeling of wildness, a sudden silence and limitless space wakens nomadic dreams in my soul. Anticipation. A sound like the sea rides the wind.

∗ ∗ ∗

The Río Grande Gorge begins as a shallow canyon near the Colorado border. From Lobatos Bridge in Colorado to Velarde

Diversion Dam in New Mexico (81.5 miles), the Río Grande is a charter member of the Wild and Scenic Rivers System. The Wild and Scenic Rivers Act protects the river from development along this stretch.

The Wild Rivers Cerro Wilderness preserves the majesty of two rivers, the Río Grande and the Red River, in their natural, free-flowing state. Ancient forests are home to 500-year-old piñon and juniper trees. Rugged, steep narrow trails descend from the canyon rim to the glorious silvery river. I drop into the deep ravine, trudging a winding rocky trail.

Eight hundred feet below the rim, I find a sandy beach, take off my rugged old boots to stretch out my swollen toes in the cool water. Carved into the boulders and cliffs are hundreds of images ranging from swirls and dots to human and animal figures. The river splashes past huge black basalt boulders worn smooth. Golden leaves whirl from the trees. Heart shaped — *the perfection of a heart shaped leaf* — they settle on shore, drift on the sparkling water.

* * *

East of the spectacular Río Grande Gorge Bridge, the rim trail crisscrosses over a broad mesa. At the edge of the mesa, the jagged rift splits the earth up close and personal, a shadowy, dark abyss. A ribbon of jade rushes past eight hundred feet below. Volcanic shapes dot the plains. The Sangre de Cristo Range leans into the sky, cradling in its great heart oceans and storm clouds, sherds and bones. Spirits still meet here in the scarlet bluffs, gathering together in the good silence of prayer.

Just off the trail, I spot a stone labyrinth, sheltered by a rough circle of boulders etched with dancing figures, figures from a time long past. A herd of sheep graze nearby. A shallow round pond mirrors the sky. I walk the narrow dirt trail that winds across the mesa. A wisdom of lichen-covered rock, sage and buried rivers whispers of other dimensions living on in intimate acquaintance with this landscape. Among the sage and serpents, ancient spirits dance in skeins of light, grounded in this wild energy of space. A drum echo calls back its people to dance. Dancers dressed in blue move in a line, as shadows. Raising dust.

* * *

Steve Harris brought his rafting company, Far Flung Adventures, from Big Bend, Texas, to Taos, New Mexico. Steve's intense passion for the Río Grande, his efforts working for the river, and his knowledge of the complex issues surrounding the river are obvious within moments of our meeting. His concerns run deep:

"Our vocabulary, our attitudes, influence our disconnect from the natural world. If we see the river in the narrowest way as *resource,* rather than a live river, it is there for human consumption. Western civilization is based on turning the natural world into commerce, domesticating or destroying all that is natural. We have forgotten that river as river has value. An economy-driven culture determines dominance over, rather than reverence for. The river is stretched thin by the dizzying pace and magnitude of water development. We don't really have a policy that protects rivers. There are few voices raised in the river's defense." Steve and I sit on the porch steps of his cabin; a forest of aspens weave their magic, gentle with the voice of a place unused to people. We listen as the river splashes by.

In Albuquerque, New Mexico, the Río Grande Nature Center is built at the edge of the river. Grand old cottonwoods grace the river corridor. Here, a sense of peace touches my spirit and emotions, a rare and vanishing thing in a world driven by distraction and noise. Cliff Crawford and I walk the trails; he speaks of the changing river:

"For millions of years, the river wandered, or plugged up. The river was a dynamic system, re-creating forest, re-creating self. Over a long time, millions of years, the river's natural cycles made it possible for riparian areas to exist. Seedlings grew in the moist soil left behind by spring floods; a mosaic of forests, open meadows and wetlands flourished. What we're looking at now is a fixed river. It's got constraints on it that it didn't have before.

"Not so long ago the Río Grande meandered across a miles-wide flood plain. Before dams, levees and jetty jacks altered the entire river system, the río ran muddy and free. Spring flooding scoured debris, leaving behind rich silty soil, pockets of wetlands and sandy beaches. Flooding is an elemental process, key to structuring riverine and riparian environments. Today we have a channel. Today the Río Grande, as well as its diverse ecology, is one of the most endangered rivers in the world."

Matt Mitchell lives south of Albuquerque near the river. He tells me, "In the morning, before light, I walk outside with my coffee. The river has a personality — a living presence, a sound for all its moods and fluctuations. I stop to listen. The river can go dry and silent, then it rains. The sound of the river may be gentle or wild or mysterious or free. We are fortunate here in Bosquecito, no levees divert the river's natural flow; the river has the potential to be a real river."

* * *

Several years ago, I worked as a watershed ecologist for the Friends of the Bosque del Apache National Wildlife Refuge in southern New Mexico. My mission in working with children was for us to create a geographical map of the Río Grande Watershed, filling in details concerning ecological health. Responsibility, respect and care, ecology, restoration and partnership formed the foundation of our studies.

We entered a world in community with fellow inhabitants — the feathered, furred and scaled. Each day we would rest on the ground by the river to read from our notebooks… the children's words were profound, filled with a sense of participation.

"I hear the water's voice calling.
I can call the river in my mind. The sun's heat is very strong,
just like the river pushing on me."

HESUS
Mapping the Río

We called upon experts in the fields of biology, ecology, soil conservation, archeology and history to work with us. We walked the hills and riverbanks. We explored wetland, forest and river habitat, as well as effects of human intervention.

"You flow so gently where you are strong.
You keep us, and the world alive. Shaping, shifting, you
make your way down the river bed. But when we stopped your
flow, and dammed you, the bad times began."

ARIEL
Mapping the Río

The Bosque del Apache NWR provided a rich laboratory for our watershed studies. The restored wetlands attract a diverse population of wildlife that would otherwise be adrift. Many birds, fish, reptiles, mammals, insects, amphibians, coyotes, bears, cougars and beavers find their permanent home here. In fall and winter, thousands of shore birds, water birds, raptors and sandhill cranes migrate from northern climates to the Middle Río Grande Valley. My students and I roamed healthy integrated systems, vibrant and full of life. We applied our scientific minds to studying bugs and wetland biology, documenting how quickly toxic and careless attitudes can destroy a fragile balance. Our notebooks were filled with drawings, observations and thoughts.

"I see the blue river rushing in a hurry.
I smell the dark brown mud. I hear the river with such
hurry rushing back to its beginning."

ANTONIO
Mapping the Río

Gina Dello Russo, a Bosque del Apache ecologist, uses the word "balance" to describe changing the perception that everything is for us. "The natural world does not circulate around us. If we, as common citizens, would take advantage of this understanding we could ask the important questions. What is possible? What is possible working with the river?"

"I see a river, and some trees and sticks with leaves,
sand and a lonely pinecone. I smell a beautiful river, and
the sweet scent of trees and wet sand. I hear a river running and

the soft wind going through the trees. I feel soft
sand and crunchy leaves and one hard stick.
I wonder why the river flows and where did it start?"

JEAN-PAUL
Mapping the Río

"Later on I realized what my message to the river was.
It was that we needed each other."

MATILDA
Mapping the Río

Big Bend

I drive south to Big Bend National Park to find…time…to hike the trails…to stand with the river…to breathe deep into wildness…

Big Bend refers to the great southwestern Texas U-turn the Río Grande makes here. According to the map, in Big Bend National Park most roads end at the Río Grande, the natural boundary between the United States and Mexico.

Río Grande — El Bravo del Norte: from its headwaters in the Colorado Rockies to its return to the sea, the mighty Río travels 1,885 miles through mountain, desert and canyon to reach the Gulf of Mexico. Río Grande, lifeblood.

A hawk soars overhead, sweeps over the mesa coasting low, great wings translucent in sunlight.

Driving, we seek the Río Grande.

On a grassy plain beneath a stand of cottonwoods, a heavyset man smokes a cigarette outside his RV. Have you walked to the river? I ask.

"River?" He looks puzzled. "What river?"

About the Author

Alexis Rykken has lived in remote areas of the Southwest for most of her adult life, captivated by wild lands, nourished by the mystery and grit of untamed country. She holds a master of education degree and works as a writer, ecologist, and educator.

Alex designed and implemented "Mapping the Río," an interdisciplinary field study of the Río Grande Watershed, and produced a DVD featuring the Río Grande. She also partnered with a San Antonio Elementary School fifth-grade class to publish a field guide featuring the Bosque del Apache National Wildlife Refuge in southern New Mexico and has worked as a volunteer with Mission:Wolf. Thinking Wilderness selected Alex as a "featured wilderness thinker" in 2014.

Of her love affair with wilderness, Alex writes, "It is here I feel connected — hand, foot, and heart — to my inner spirit, to Earth's dream, to my own dream for Earth."